THE TAMPA TRIBUNE

PEWTER POWER
The Bucs' Unforgettable Championship Season

TRIUMPH
BOOKS
CHICAGO

THE TAMPA TRIBUNE

Steven M. Weaver   Publisher, President
Gil Thelen   Senior Vice President, Executive Editor
Kermit J. Kauffman   Vice President of Finance
Donna R. Reed   Managing Editor
Amy Chown   Marketing Director

BOOK CREDITS
Senior Editor/Sports: Richard "Duke" Maas
Editor: Rick Mayer
Designer: Ray Ramos
Copy Editor: Tom Brew
Writers: Roy Cummings, Mick Elliott, Martin Fennelly,
Carter Gaddis, Joe Henderson, Joey Johnston, Ira Kaufman,
Katherine Smith
Photo Editors: Todd Chappel, Joseph Brown
Photographers: Jason Behnken, Cliff McBride, David
Kadlubowski, Scott Iskowitz
Photo Assistance: Greg Williams

ON THE COVER: Jon Gruden hoists the Lombardi Trophy after his team's convincing victory over the Oakland Raiders in Super Bowl XXXVII. By David Kadlubowski of *The Tampa Tribune*.

ON THE TITLE PAGE: John Lynch celebrates a Bucs touchdown against the Green Bay Packers on Nov. 24. By David Kadlubowski of The Tampa Tribune.

For fanatical coverage of the Tampa Bay Buccaneers, read *The Tampa Tribune*, go to TBO.com (Keyword: Bucs) and watch WFLA, News Channel 8. For home delivery of *The Tampa Tribune*, call (813) 874-2863 or 1-800-282-5588.

Printed in the United States of America

CONTENTS

Bucs 48, Raiders 21
January 26 at San Diego

Champions of the World

By JOEY JOHNSTON

For a half-dozen seasons, the Lombardi Trophy seemed within reach. But it never was close enough to touch.

The Bucs, with their annual collection of Pro Bowlers, were derisively described as "paper champions." Talented enough to qualify for the NFL's postseason, yes, but unable to make a serious run at the title.

Fair or not, it became the organization's reputation. Everyone came to believe that about the Bucs. Paper champions. Good, but never great.

That perception is history. The Bucs are champions . . . period. Rip up the paper into tiny pieces. Replace it with stainless steel, the kind that is used to manufacture a glistening Lombardi Trophy.

"I've dreamed of this moment," Bucs linebacker Derrick Brooks said as he caressed the NFL's most tangible prize. "It's amazing that it's actually happened. But you know what? We deserved it."

They were the real champions, the genuine article. A team that played its best in the clutch. Players who unabashedly went on the road, in subfreezing temperatures, and ripped the heart out of an entire city. Coaches who pushed all the right buttons and devised schemes to confound the opposition.

GAME SUMMARY

Raiders	3	0	6	12	- 21
Bucs	3	17	14	14	- 48

First Quarter

O - FG Janikowski 40, 10:40. Drive: 7 plays, 14 yards, 2:55.
TB - FG Gramatica 31, 7:51. Drive, 9 plays, 58 yards, 2:49.

Second Quarter

TB - FG Gramatica 43, 11:16. Drive: 9 plays, 26 yards, 3:53.
TB - Alstott 2 run (Gramatica kick), 6:24. Drive: 4 plays, 27 yards, 2:02.
TB - McCardell 5 pass from B. Johnson (Gramatica kick), 0:30. Drive: 10 plays, 77 yards, 3:15.

Third Quarter

TB - McCardell 8 pass from B. Johnson (Gramatica kick), 4:30. Drive 14 plays, 89 yards, 7:52.
TB - Smith 44 interception return (Gramatica kick), 4:47.
O - Porter 39 pass from Gannon (pass failed), 2:14. Drive: 8 plays, 82 yards, 2:33.

Fourth Quarter

O - Johnson 13 return of blocked punt (pass failed), 14:16.
O - Rice 48 pass from Gannon (pass failed), 6:06. Drive: 8 play, 78 yards, 2:58.
TB - Brooks 44 interception return (Gramatica kick), 1:18.
TB - Smith 50 interception return (Gramatica kick), 0:02.
A - 67,603

REACTION

"[Gruden] wouldn't say it, but we knew he wanted to beat the Raiders and stick it to them the first time he got a chance. . . . Everybody who thought we weren't going to do it, stick it in their face."—Keyshawn Johnson

REACTION

"I never got down on myself. The offense was a work in progress. I kept believing, pounding the rock and I knew good things would happen." —Michael Pittman, who had his best day as a Buc in the Super Bowl, running for 124 yards.

NUMBERS GAME

The Raiders' offense managed only four first downs through the first 41 minutes of the game. The team finished with 11 first downs, only one by rushing.

HIGHEST SCORING SUPER BOWLS

SB	Result	Points
XXIX	49ers 49, Chargers 26	75
XXXVII	Bucs 48, Raiders 21	69
XXVII	Dallas 52, Bills 17	69
XIII	Steelers 35, Cowboys 31	66
XXIV	49ers 55, Broncos 10	65
XXVI	Redskins 37, Bills 24	61

BUCS 48, RAIDERS 21

These were the facts. The Bucs found themselves dancing on the floor of San Diego's Qualcomm Stadium, with red and white confetti being sprayed in celebration. This was reality. And there was no doubt, especially from the vanquished Oakland Raiders.

The Bucs had pounded the Raiders 48–21 in Super Bowl XXXVII, completing one of the most impressive postseason runs in recent NFL history. Bucs coach Jon Gruden had beaten his old team, the Raiders, who desperately wanted to teach him a lesson. The Tampa Bay defense, which registered five interceptions to set a Super Bowl record, could now take its rightful place among the Steel Curtain, the 1985 Bears and the 2000 Ravens.

There were sentimental scenes, like the defensive veterans—Brooks, defensive tackle Warren Sapp and safety John Lynch—the ones who had been around the longest, gleefully running around the sideline like they were little kids at the playground. There were unexpected heroes like free safety Dexter Jackson, the Super Bowl's Most Valuable Player, who had two interceptions, and nickel back Dwight Smith, who returned two more interceptions for touchdowns.

The only paper for these champions came from the red and white confetti that poured from the brim of Qualcomm Stadium.

Among the stories of redemption was the one from Pittman (32), who shredded the Raiders' defense for a season-high 124 yards. Alstott (40) blocked effectively and scored the game's first touchdown.

There were stories of redemption, like the one from running back Michael Pittman, a free-agent who had struggled mightily and failed to give Tampa Bay a needed marquee running threat during the regular season. But he claimed vindication after shredding the Raiders for a season-high 124 yards.

There was the feeling of satisfaction from Tampa Bay's much-maligned offensive line, which peaked at the proper time and didn't allow a sack of quarterback Brad Johnson when stakes were the highest.

And what about Johnson himself? In his 13th season, he never was anyone's choice to become an elite quarterback. Yet in the Super Bowl, he overcame a slow start and threw a pair of touchdown passes to Keenan McCardell.

Perhaps it's fitting that every Tampa Bay player will receive a miniature version of the Lombardi Trophy. They each did a little bit to make this happen.

"Words can't describe what I'm feeling right now," said Gruden, who, at age 39, became the youngest coach ever to win a Super Bowl.

Could anything accurately describe how a season goes from promising to special to magical?

How did they get here?

This precious moment once was unimaginable. Bucs in the Super Bowl? Bucs WINNING the Super Bowl?

Are you kidding?

The Bucs once were so inept, they lost 26 consecutive games as an expansion team, testing the wisecracking resolve of inaugural coach John McKay, before finally breaking through with the franchise's initial victory. They were so hopeless, premium draft picks were spent on Bo Jackson (who played baseball instead), Booker Reese, Keith McCants and Eric Curry.

They were so laughable, several players were ashamed to wear those old orange creamsicle jerseys and helmets with the winking pirate logo. They were so ironically out of place, three of their banished quarterbacks (Doug Williams, Steve Young and Trent Dilfer) actually won Super Bowl MVP awards for other teams.

"I'm not lying to you, it was a third-world country," Sapp said.

So how did they get here?

The foundation was laid by Tony Dungy, the former coach who built the Bucs into respectability with four playoff appearances in five seasons. But that wasn't enough. In the words of Steelers defensive back Lee Flowers, the Bucs were nothing more than "paper champions," a collection of Pro Bowlers who curled up during the big games.

The Bucs were part of the Super Bowl limelight, which included the usual pregame pageantry.

Dungy was a warm glass of milk.

A spark? What the Bucs needed most was a shot glass of battery acid.

They got Jon Gruden.

And almost immediately, they began pounding the rock.

The Bucs paid some compensation ransom—two number one draft picks, two number two picks and $8 million—in order to pry Gruden away from the Raiders. What they got was a coach with the nocturnal habits of a hamster. What they got was an attitude.

"You either feel pressure or you apply it." That was Gruden's proclamation upon his arrival in Tampa. And it was clear that nothing ever would be the same.

The emotional Gruden got pumped up while watching Smith's interception return.

Tampa Bay's offensive line did a super job, allowing no sacks against Brad Johnson.

Gramatica kicked two field goals to open the Bucs' scoring. Then he kept reappearing for all those extra points.

Both of McCardell's receptions went for touchdowns, and the second catch put the Bucs up 27–3.

Easygoing comfort was replaced by heated urgency. Holdover assistants, who whispered through their routines, morphed into shouting and sprinting.

The Bucs were going somewhere. And they were getting there in a hurry. That was obvious in the early minicamps. It was confirmed when the Bucs convened for training camp at Disney's Wide World of Sports. The team had a plan. Slackers weren't tolerated.

No longer content to kick a few field goals and leave it for the defense, Tampa Bay aimed for game-winning contributions everywhere. From the opening practice, Gruden challenged his offense to keep up. He demanded that his star defenders, already established NFL superstars, not settle for anything less than number one status.

Gruden's version of the West Coast offense was implemented. The new terminology was something akin to learning to speak Spanish and French simultaneously. It stumbled and struggled through the early season, remaining a work in progress. Then it took off during the postseason, employing all the weapons from Keyshawn Johnson to Mike Alstott to Ken Dilger to Joe Jurevicius.

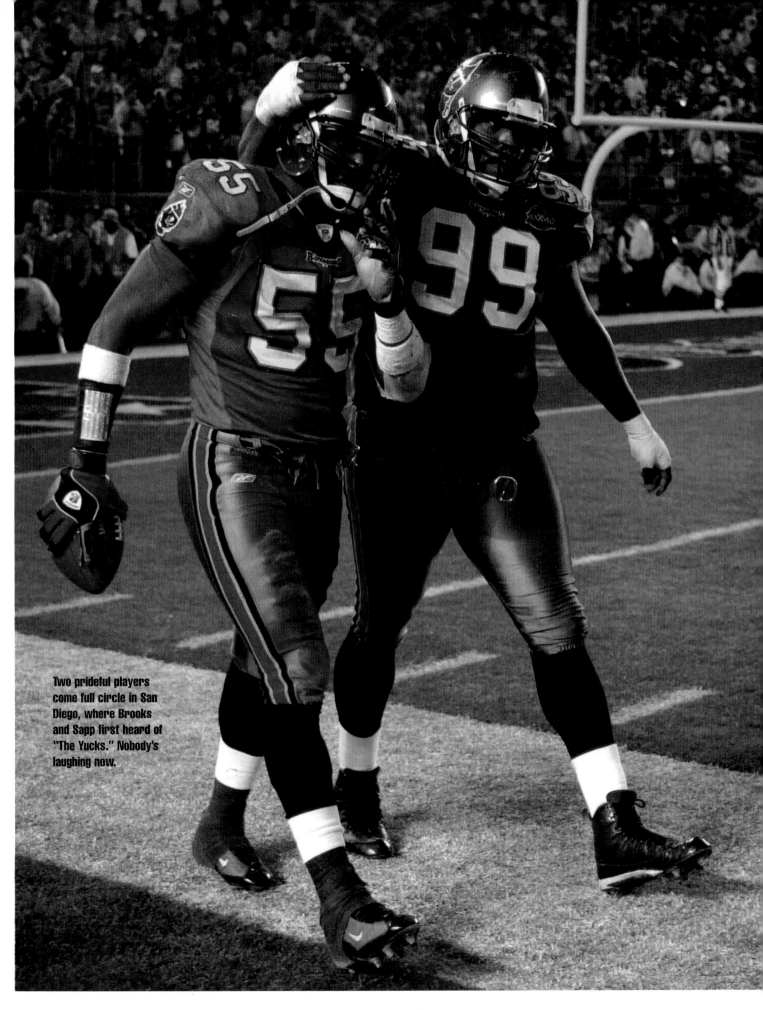

Two prideful players come full circle in San Diego, where Brooks and Sapp first heard of "The Yucks." Nobody's laughing now.

Defensive coordinator Monte Kiffin's squad was redoubtable, as always. But now, it was even better. Gruden's fire rubbed off. The successful conversion of Shelton Quarles to middle linebacker made it a faster overall unit. Brooks chased greatness. Sapp and Lynch played to their Pro Bowl levels. Quote-machine Simeon Rice hovered near Mars with his pregame poetry, but grounded himself into the pocket to menace opposing quarterbacks. On the corners, Ronde Barber and Brian Kelly were huge playmakers.

There was symmetry to Tampa Bay's season. They were 6–2 in each half, 3–1 in each quarter. For the NFC Championship Game, they returned to Philadelphia, the site of previous postseason disaster. The hump that they couldn't cross. But in a spirited reversal of form, the Bucs closed down the Vet and beat the Eagles 27–10, applying an exclamation mark with Barber's late 92-yard interception return.

Before that game, somebody spotted a large bottle of champagne, on ice, being wheeled into the Eagles' executive offices. That party never happened. The Bucs were on their way to

In deserving fashion, Brooks' interception thwarted a Raiders rally and sealed the win.

Two sacks by Rice helped the Bucs' defense keep pressure on the Raiders, even with a big lead.

the Super Bowl. And as Sapp said, they didn't just go for the trip.

"You want to be considered one of the best teams ever to play this game," Sapp said. "Our stats say we are. But our fingers don't say we are. No rings. We've got to do something about that."

So in the city of San Diego, the very place in 1996 where Sapp and Brooks heard ESPN refer to the team as "the Yucks," thus lighting a fire underneath the two prideful players, things came full circle.

In a way, it was all so difficult to believe. But in another way, maybe not. There was the Lombardi Trophy. Now it belonged to the Bucs. No one was afraid to touch it. It's easy to believe in something you can see and feel.

This time, it was real. And this time, the Bucs really were champions of the world.

Jackson's two interceptions turned the momentum in Tampa Bay's favor. The Super Bowl MVP's first pick set up a field goal that put the Bucs ahead for good.

The Quiet Chief

By CARTER GADDIS

"There's a lot of Indians, but there's no chiefs over there. . . . And I'm not quite sure they have the guy that can really step up and be a leader." —Former Bucs linebacker Hardy Nickerson in October 2000

Hardy Nickerson wasn't being vindictive. It wasn't sour grapes. As far as he could tell, his former team was rudderless, leaderless, hopeless without him.

Without his considerable presence, he reasoned, his old teammates were adrift. No purpose. No discipline. No chief.

What Nickerson did not take into account at the time was that leadership takes many forms in an NFL locker room. While Nickerson was the fiery, energetic type—the kind of veteran player who made sure everyone knew exactly whose locker room they were in— there was another Pro Bowl linebacker at One Buc Place who had other ideas about what it means to lead.

If Warren Sapp is the heart of the Bucs' number one-ranked defense, if John Lynch is its cerebral center, if Simeon Rice is its mouthpiece, if Ronde Barber is its spirit, then Derrick Brooks is its soul.

In a locker room brimming with personality, in a place where no microphone is ignored for long, Brooks has over the years quietly become the chief that Nickerson didn't know was there.

The NFL Defensive Player of the Year has done so without the demonstrativeness of Nickerson, but every bit as effectively.

"I think when I first got here [in 1997], he was more a leader-by-example guy," Barber said. "'I'll just go out and do my job, and if you want to be friends with me you can, but you don't have to. Just work with me.'

"That's when Hardy was here, and he was the big leader on defense. Hardy left, and it just developed into Derrick's defense. He's the leader. Whenever there's a conflict or whatever's going on with the defense, he's always up there at the wheel."

Nickerson wasn't there to witness the evolution of Brooks. He saw the quiet Brooks, the lead-by-example Brooks, the Brooks whose play on the field was inspiring but whose locker room presence was much more subtle.

Away from the field, confrontation wasn't Brooks' style. Who had time for confrontation when there was work to be done?

Brooks, much like Nickerson, shows up early and goes home late. Film work, weight work, study, run it in practice and run it again.

For a young player such as middle linebacker Shelton Quarles, Brooks was a guiding force.

"Both him and Hardy," Quarles said. "When I first came here in 1997, I got to see the kind of person you should be as a football player. They're always on the field, they're always lifting weights, they're always going that extra step, they're always watching film. I think that showed me what I need to do and how I need to be as a player. He was an excellent role model coming into the system."

He'll talk when he has to. Even as Nickerson gave his faraway critique that fall of 2000, even as the Bucs limped through the early portion of the 2000 season, Brooks began to assert himself as the vocal leader.

After consecutive losses to the Jets and Redskins, as he watched his teammates mope around the locker room, Brooks ordered the doors closed. He spoke. They listened.

"We're 3–2," Brooks said. "If you're not hungry for a win so bad now, you don't need to be part of this ballclub. And that's as clear-cut as I can get."

Fast forward to October 27, 2002, against the unimposing Carolina Panthers. It took three long-range field goals by Martin Gramatica to make one of Tampa Bay's best defensive performances of the year stand up.

And stand up is exactly what Brooks urged his emotionally drained teammates to do as Gramatica lined up for the game-winning, 47-yard kick with five seconds left.

"Get up!" Brooks implored as he sprinted along the sideline. "Get up here and watch us win this game!"

Brooks was one of the first players Gruden wanted to meet when he was hired to replace Tony Dungy. Brooks came into Gruden's office and sat down.

"He sort of stared at me for about 30 seconds before he said anything," Brooks said. "I was like, 'What's up with this dude?'

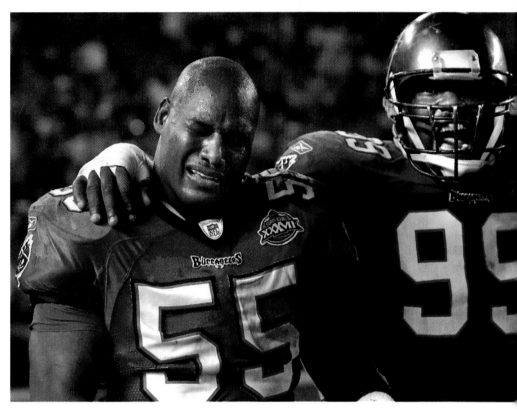

All the hard work paid off for Brooks, who rained tears of joy as the Bucs' reign began.

"He stared at me and I said, 'Welcome. Glad you're here.'

"He said straight at me, 'I'm going to need you. I'm going to need you to lead this football team.'

"He told me everything he heard about me was well-deserved and that he was looking for a lot more from me to get this team going. It was going to be key in his mind that I do it because he knew the loyalty this team had for coach Dungy. Me being a leader for this defense, he wanted to make sure that I was focused. . . .

"Obviously, [there were] a lot of old feelings, the manner in which coach Dungy left the organization. All that being said, there were a lot of hurt feelings, but we're professionals. You lick your wounds and you move on."

Brooks responded to the challenge by having the best of

his eight seasons. His four touchdowns on turnovers (three on interceptions, one on a fumble recovery) tied for the second-most in NFL history. He led the team in tackles with 170, extending his team record for tackles to 1,277. He led all NFL linebackers with 15 defended passes and was named to the Pro Bowl for the sixth consecutive season.

"He's a true professional," Quarles said. "He shows up every day. He works hard. And he tries to put his best foot forward with every practice. . . . I think he's evolved into an excellent leader. He knows what to say and when to say it."

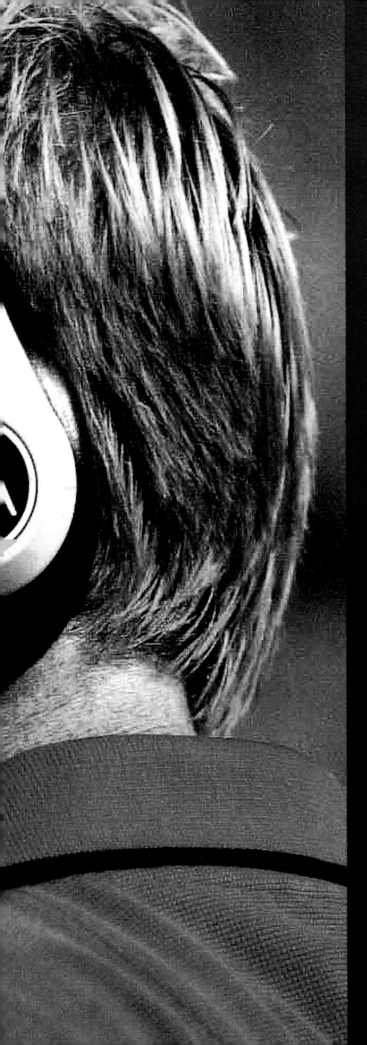

One Morning with a Genius

T he road is empty. In the darkness, you hear bullfrogs croaking in the drainage ditch across the street from One Chucky Place.

The man in the security booth phones the man in the cave. "Jon, this is Charlie. That guy is here." Charlie leads the way. He raps on a door.

"What is that?" says the voice behind the door. Jon Gruden's 6:00 A.M. appointment is 15 minutes early. Gruden, having risen at the appointed hour—and minute—arrived at 4:00 A.M.

Since then, he's been sitting in his office, the one he ordered built without windows, drawing play cards for practice. What light there is comes from a small table lamp, the powder blue glow of a computer and a TV screen displaying the New Orleans Saints in their goal-line defense.

Across two grease boards on the wall in front of Gruden's desk is the hour-by-hour schedule for the

plays and a few phone numbers, including one with the word "home" next to it, so Gruden remembers when he tries to ring back to the house in which he lives.

He is drawing. Play after play. Lines everywhere. Go routes, post routes, blast plays, blocking assignments. He switches out colored markers and pens and applies his best friend, Wite-Out. He tosses aside one play sheet and starts another.

He is talking and drawing. It's hard to believe, as fast as those pens are racing, that these are the plays . . . these are the plays to save the Bucs offense. You notice that the sheets Gruden uses come with circles for the offensive line already stenciled on.

"That's too bad, because I am a hell of a circle drawer," Gruden says. "I practiced drawing circles when I was younger. I wanted to be good on the board. Know what I mean? I wanted to be a good circle drawer."

He smiled.

"You got to get it right, bro."

Here is Gruden, 39, already on his fifth pro team, with millions guaranteed. Here he is, one of the 50 most beautiful circle drawers, scribbling before dawn, racing those pens, racing that clock.

He's in shirt, shorts and socks. Those markers and pens keep smoking, the sheets keep flying. The sun is hours away. It's why people who love Gruden worry about him. And burnout.

"I ain't going there," he said. "I like what I do. Everybody talks about how Dick Vermeil was burned out. That blows my mind. Dick Vermeil came back when he was 60 years old. Not once, but twice. Give me a break."

He draws a running play. It's 6:25.

"I don't really know about a lot of things in the world. I'm not proud of it. I don't know who the hell this Greenspan guy is. The war with Iraq? Don't know. I'm one of those guys who reads the headlines, doesn't read the story. I'm informed, but I have no knowledge. Know what I mean, man?"

He grabs the Wite-Out. That wideout doesn't go there. Things have to be just right. Not for nothing do people call Gruden an offensive genius.

The genius has lost his wallet 10 times during the past three years. When his wife, Cindy, bless her soul, calls him, she makes sure to repeat her cell number.

"It's never 'Call me,'" Jon says. "Always has to give me the number. Knows I don't remember. Is that a genius? That's a moron for you."

He stacks plays, grabs more paper.

"Maybe it's insecurity, how much I work. Maybe a little. I just hate to waste a year. I just hate to waste time. I can't stand that. I hate to see guys—OK, maybe I'm guilty of overdoing it—but these guys with their 'I'll get it next year.' Next year. Next week. Next down.

"Bull. We're going to lose this game if you don't do it right. We're going to get this done. Today. Now."

He finishes up another play.

"I'm not worried about consequences. I'm not worried about failure. Know what I'm saying? If I'm not good enough, I'll find another job. Hell, I'll work for the *Tribune*. I'll deliver newspapers. I'm up early. I ain't afraid to work. I don't expect these guys to be afraid of it, either."

He shakes a red marker. It's dying from use.

"Some guys don't respond to getting their butts ripped. You got to know who you're yelling at. Know what I mean? I've been accused of being Harry High School, yelling too much. But maybe this is something I do well. Maybe a guy might say: 'I never liked that sucker, but at least I knew where he was coming from.'

"If you're going to card every play for practice, to give your team a look, don't just come in at 8:00 A.M. and do a [lousy] job. All you can do is the best you can do."

The computer hums.

"I spend a lot of time in this dark room. No distractions. I think we're all like that. Maybe me more. I've always been a loner, bro. It's a bad thing in some ways. Because loners are lonely. Doesn't it seem a little lonely in here?"

He thinks of his so-far-so-fast career.

"I haven't done much yet."

He draws another play.

"My dad told me something one time. I was in Philadelphia, moaning about something. Dad says: 'Why don't you quit complaining? Why don't you go to a cemetery and look at all the rocks? Some people have been under those rocks a hundred years. One day, you'll be under one.'

"That's a hell of a thing. It tells you: we've got to, somewhere, some way, max out—get all you can get out of your days."

Gruden grimaces at {the ultimate form of inactivity.

"I'm not a real good guy when it comes to death. I don't deal with it good. It's over. The game is over. I believe in God and go to church, but death, man, it bothers me. Maybe that's a motivation in a lot of ways. You just got to keep thumping."

He opens his door. It's 8:00 A.M.

"Man, it's light out," Gruden says. "You never know it when you're in there. You never know, bro."

"Not everybody is going to be like I am. But I believe in urgency. I believe in tempo. I believe in finishing."

Road to the Super Bowl

The Bucs made the world forget about the past by rewriting their record book and closing the joke book that followed them for most of their 27 seasons. They had the NFL's top-rated defense and quarterback, a 1,000-yard receiver and the league leader in interceptions. They featured five Pro Bowlers while setting a team standard for victories. They won in the cold and closed the Vet with a bang! Their coach was a celebrity with as much smile and scowl. Oh, and they had the NFL's defensive MVP—some guy named Brooks! To keep those memories fresh, relive the greatest season in Tampa Bay history on the following pages through the eyes of the reporters who covered it.

McAfee came marching into the endzone, and Tupa's desparation toss was picked off for the game-winning score

Saints 26, **Bucs 20**
September 8 at Tampa

A Rotten Start

Part of the idea behind hiring Jon Gruden was to make fans forget about the past. During his regular-season debut against the New Orleans Saints, Gruden and his charges could only conjure memories of it.

For three quarters, a span in which the Bucs gained 161 yards of total offense, Gruden's Bucs looked a lot like the 1996 Bucs that started the season 1–7.

There also were times during this 26–20 loss, most notably during a second-half rally, in which a stifling defense and a suddenly efficient offense forced overtime, when Gruden's team looked like the division-winning Bucs of 1999.

"We probably shot ourselves in the foot a couple of times today," left tackle Roman Oben said.

No bullet struck deeper than the one punter Tom Tupa took in the waning moments of overtime. Standing deep in his own end zone, the right-handed Tupa first failed to avoid a right-side bull rush by the Saints' Fred McAfee, then tried to save a broken play by tossing the ball.

Someone asked Tupa which one of his teammates was the intended receiver. "Anyone," Tupa said.

The ball never made it out of the end zone. As Tupa was taken down by McAfee,

---

GAME SUMMARY

Saints	6	7	7	0	6 - 26
Bucs	0	3	7	10	0 - 20

First Quarter
NO - FG Carney 28, 8:13. Drive: 13 plays, 65 yards, 6:47.
NO - FG Carney 41, :19. Drive: 11 plays, 51 yards, 4:40.

Second Quarter
TB - FG Gramatica 52, 13:20. Drive: 6 plays, 39 yards, 1:59.
NO - B.Williams 32 pass from A.Brooks (Carney kick), 4:02. Drive: 7 plays, 64 yards, 4:22.

Third Quarter
TB - McCardell 4 pass from B.Johnson (Gramatica kick), 11:34. Drive: 6 plays, 54 yards, 3:26.
NO - Stallworth 41 pass from A.Brooks (Carney kick), 8:36. Drive: 6 plays, 82 yards, 2:58.

Fourth Quarter
TB - Jurevicious 11 pass from B.Johnson (Gramatica kick), 2:41. Drive: 12 plays, 73 yards, 2:29.
TB - FG Gramatica 40, :00. Drive 10 plays, 51 yards, 2:01.
Overtime
NO - Allen interception in end zone, 2:50.
A - 65,554.

REACTION
" We will learn from this." —Warren Sapp

NUMBERS GAME
The Bucs are 10-11-1 in regular-season overtime games, including 6-3-1 at home.

BUCS COACHING DEBUTS

Year	Coach	Opponent	Result
1976	John McKay	at Houston	Lost, 20-0
1985	Leeman Bennett	at Chicago	Lost, 38-28
1987	Ray Perkins	Atlanta	Won, 48-10
1990	Richard Williamson*	Minnesota	Won, 26-13
1992	Sam Wyche	Phoenix	Won, 23-7
1996	Tony Dungy	Green Bay	Lost, 34-3
2002	Jon Gruden	New Orleans	Lost, 26-20

* Williamson's first game was the 14th game of the season.

NFC SOUTH STANDINGS

	W	L	T
Carolina	1	0	0
New Orleans	1	0	0
Tampa Bay	0	1	0
Atlanta	0	1	0

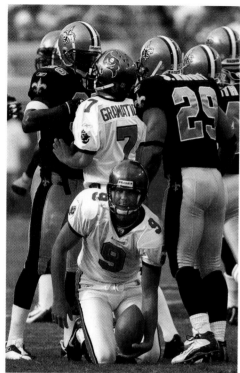

New Orleans blocked a field goal just before halftime, but Gramatica and the Bucs did not back down.

Down by 10, McCardell started Tampa Bay's comeback with a third-quarter touchdown.

linebacker James Allen picked off Tupa's shovel pass for the game-winning touchdown.

The Bucs gained fewer yards rushing (72) than they surrendered in penalties (85), missed one field-goal try and had another blocked. Their two top receivers combined to catch eleven passes and drop three, including two on third down, and their quarterback was sacked three times and hit many times more.

"All those flags, those penalties, those plays, they may not show up in the stat sheet," Gruden said. "But they were costly. And I'm disappointed. But I'm not going to let this one fester for very long. We have a good football team and we're going to come back from this."

Led by the elusive Aaron Brooks, the Saints gained 203 total yards and seemingly underachieved by scoring 13 points while controlling the ball for 21 minutes in the first half.

In the second half, the Bucs' defense did a better job of giving the ball back to the offense. They forced the Saints to punt the ball away on each of their last five possessions. In turn, the

offense did a better job of putting the ball in the end zone.

The Bucs tied the game on an 11-yard Brad Johnson touchdown pass to Joe Jurevicius and a 40-yard Martin Gramatica field goal as regulation ended.

Both offenses were guilty of pressing in overtime. The Saints gained 21 yards on 9 plays while the Bucs gained 27 on 15.

"It became a battle of field position, and we lost it," cornerback Ronde Barber said.

Late in overtime, when Karl Williams retrieved a punt at his own 10 and was taken down at his 6, the end seemed inevitable.

"We had a lot of mental errors; we had a lot of chances at the end of the game to win," receiver Keenan McCardell said. "We had our opportunities, but we gave it away."

Roy Cummings

Showing no signs of age and with a "chip on his shoulder," Brooks ran and ran and ran, 97 yards to the end zone.

Bucs 25, Ravens 0
September 15 at Baltimore

Golden Oldies

Derrick Brooks ran. He had batted a pass, grabbed the ball and ran. He ran 97 yards. He was mad the whole way. He'd been mad the whole week.

"There's no mistake about it . . . we played with a little chip on our shoulder," Brooks said. "They say we're getting old, this, that and the other. I get a little angry."

They all got a little angry. They all got a little even. Tucked in Brooks' arm was an intercepted ball, believed to be the one pass not swatted away by Ronde Barber. Brooks carried a 25–0 shutout to the end zone.

A shutout is a shutout is a shutout. It doesn't matter who it's against. Before playing Baltimore, the Bucs played 406 games in their 27-year history. This was their fifth shutout. A shutout always matters.

"We're a prideful group," John Lynch said.

It didn't matter that the Baltimore Ravens were suddenly awful, or that Ravens quarterback Chris Redman was starting just his second NFL game or that Baltimore's offense marked the passing of John Unitas by observing 60 minutes of silence.

But you can't overestimate what a game like this meant to the Bucs' defense and to this team. It had spent the first

---

GAME SUMMARY

Bucs	10	3	5	7	- 25
Ravens	0	0	0	0	- 0

First Quarter
TB - FG Gramatica 36, 7:39. Drive: 12 plays, 60 yards, 7:21
TB - K.Williams 56 punt return (Gramatica kick), 1:54.

Second Quarter
TB - FG Gramatica 30, 3:51. Drive: 17 plays, 82 yards, 8:25.

Third Quarter
TB - Safety, Redman fumble out of end zone, 14:44.
TB - FG Gramatica 30, 8:13. Drive: 11 plays, 48 yards, 6:31.

Fourth Quarter
TB - D.Brooks 97 interception return (Gramatica kick), 1:06.
A - 69,304.

REACTION
"He sent a good message. I tell you what, he had a Knute Rockne night. Oh boy, I loved it. Man, I was ready to play."
—defensive coordinator Monte Kiffin on Gruden's Saturday night speech to the team

NUMBERS GAME
The Ravens averaged 2.8 yards per play and converted only 4 of their 15 first downs.

THEY COULD GO . . .
The five longest plays in Bucs history, each resulting in a touchdown:

Date	Yds.	How they did it
Oct. 7, 2001	98	Shelton Quarles interception return vs. Green Bay
Sept. 15, 2002	97	Derrick Brooks interception return vs. Baltimore
Sept. 13, 1998	95	Jacquez Green punt return vs. Green Bay
Jan. 19, 2003	92	Ronde Barber interception return vs. Philadelphia
Dec. 2, 1990	89	Willie Drewrey pass from Vinny Testaverde vs. Atlanta

NFC SOUTH STANDINGS

	W	L	T
Carolina	2	0	0
New Orleans	2	0	0
Tampa Bay	1	1	0
Atlanta	0	2	0

BUCS 25, RAVENS 0

Quarles and Barber wrapped up the Ravens' Jamal Lewis and the Bucs limited Baltimore to 55 yards rushing. Quarles said the defense took the previous week's loss as a slap in the face.

week of this season on its heels, waiting for the Saints to make first downs on third downs, waiting to get pushed around. Sunday, the defense pushed back.

Barber, who got his mitts on another six balls to kill another six pass plays, thought back to New Orleans.

"We got hit with a right and damn near knocked out in the first round," he said. "But we buckled up and showed people what we were about today."

Defensive coordinator Monte Kiffin trudged off the field at Ravens Stadium pumping a fist without raising it.

Responding to wounded pride, Sapp's Bucs threw out the "old, predictable goose egg." It was only the fifth shutout in team history.

The Bucs put the game away early on Karl Williams' 56-yard punt return. Then the defense added points with a safety and an interception return.

"Anybody who thinks John Lynch is too old to play, or Brooks, or Sapp, they need to take a good look at this tape," Kiffin said.

The pride had been wounded.

Warren Sapp winked.

"They called us old and predictable last week," Sapp said. "So I guess we can throw the old, predictable goose egg."

John Lynch . . . he of the lost step, too old, etc. . . . wore a youthful grin. He remembered what Gruden told his team on the eve of his first win as Bucs coach. The defense ate it up. Then it ate up the Ravens.

"He told us to go out and kick somebody's [butt]" Lynch said.

It was special. A shutout is a shutout is a shutout. Linebacker Shelton Quarles thought of the previous Sunday.

"We were challenged in a major way," he said. "Sometimes that's good. It slaps you awake."

And stirs your pride.

There's no mistake about it.

Martin Fennelly

BUCCANEERS 26
RAMS 14

Sapp walked the walk after the Bucs' held the explosive Rams to less than 20 points for the third time

Bucs **26**, Rams 14
September 24 at Tampa

Monday Night Swagger

T he St. Louis Rams tried their best to show everyone at Raymond James Stadium that they were those old Rams, those swaggering Rams, those champion Rams.

So they danced on the Bucs' logo at midfield before *Monday Night Football* began. They were 0–2, and they were a desperate crew, but they wanted to show everyone they were still the Rams.

No, they weren't.

The Bucs made sure of it. They were tougher.

You knew it as Derrick Brooks carried yet another interception to the end zone, this time to save a victory, not a shutout. It was his first play back after a cramped hamstring put him on the side.

You knew it when Brooks' lead blocker on the play that sealed a 26–14 win, Warren Sapp, made a pancake filled with St. Louis quarterback Kurt Warner, the very symbol of the old Rams.

Yeah, the Bucs made sure.

And maybe picked up a little swagger of their own.

How much can you really make out of three strides of a 16-game marathon? Yes, the Bucs' offense still looked more than shaky, though the defense often looked harder than granite. Monday was important.

REACTION

"Our defense was just dominating in the second half. I think that became obvious to America." —Jon Gruden

NUMBERS GAME

Against the Rams, Brad Johnson broke Trent Dilfer's team record of 152 consecutive passes without an interception.

BUCS AT RAYMOND JAMES STADIUM

Tampa Bay has the third-best regular-season home record in the NFL since 1999 at 24-8.

Year	Regular Season	Playoffs
1998	6-2	0-0
1999	7-1	1-0
2000	6-2	0-0
2001	5-3	0-0
2002	6-2	1-0
Totals	30-10	2-0

NFC SOUTH STANDINGS

	W	L	T
Carolina	3	0	0
New Orleans	3	0	0
Tampa Bay	2	1	0
Atlanta	1	2	0

With less than a minute left in the first half, Dudley scored Tampa Bay's first touchdown in his first game as a Buc.

For Brooks, the end zone was becoming familiar territory. He returned from a hamstring injury just in time to save the game.

Here's one reason why: since 1990, 59 NFL teams began the season 0–3. Of those 59, only three advanced to the playoffs.

There you had it.

The Rams were down. The Bucs kept them down.

It's tough putting away a team hanging from a cliff, a defending NFC champion turned cornered animal.

The Rams used to get away with mistakes because of sheer talent. Now they can't cover Rickey Dudley, the new tight end who scored the Bucs' first touchdown after Simeon Rice got hit in the numbers with a Warner interception. Also in there was a great fingertip grab by Keyshawn Johnson.

Other guys have talent, too.

The Bucs sometimes get by on sheer talent, though they've never gotten by all the way to the Super Bowl. Something always stops them, usually sooner than later.

Maybe the Rams won't be that something. But there are plenty of others out there. Like Philadelphia. The torch has passed.

The Bucs' only offensive points came on a short Mike Alstott bull-rush touchdown set up by an interception by Brian Kelly, the same Brian Kelly beaten by Warner and Ricky Proehl for the game-winner in the 1999 NFC title game.

But this night wasn't for poetic justice. It was for toughness,

After Kurt Warner dropped the ball, Quarles dropped Warner and the Rams to 0–3.

toughness that overcame the offense, which missed the two-pointer after the Alstott score and rolled over after the defense finally relented. It was 19–14. Rams ball. Late fourth quarter, but plenty of time left.

The Bucs said different. The defense said different. Since 1999, the Rams have been held under 20 points only eight times. The Bucs have done it three of those times.

Brooks made sure of it. He had strained his left hamstring late in the third quarter. You could see him stretching on the side, trying to make it right. Then he went in and made a touchdown. Sapp saw Warner. The Buc leveled the Ram. One swagger was gone. Had another arrived?

Martin Fennelly

Bucs 35, Bengals 7
September 30 at Cincinnati

Easy Like Sunday Morning

Letdown? The only Bucs letdown anyone at Paul Brown Stadium witnessed was the Bucs' offense letting its hair down.

Though it still has a tendency to be conservative, there were times during the easy 35–7 pasting of the Bengals when the Bucs' offense looked downright uninhibited.

You wanted downfield passing? You got downfield passing.

Long after quarterback Brad Johnson tossed 35- and 65-yard touchdown bombs to spark the rout midway through the second quarter, the Bucs continued throwing and throwing deep.

BUCS BONUS
Just Passing Through

Offense Opens Up Playbook In 35-7 Rout Of Bengals

This Game Was Supposed To Be Easy, And It Was

"We definitely took some shots," Jon Gruden said. "I mean, we saw a team today that was intent on applying a lot of pressure, running a lot of blitzes. And that's usually how it is when you play a team that blitzes a lot. You're going to make some plays. The big thing is, we saw a different kind of defense today."

So did the Bengals. A year after it allowed Cincinnati to hang around before pulling out a 16–13 overtime win, Tampa Bay came out firing, limiting the Bengals to 168 total yards and no offensive scores.

"It was a challenge for us," Warren Sapp said. "We came up here a year ago and this team was putting on 15-play

First Quarter
Cin - Simmons 51 interception return (Rackers kick), 2:23.

Second Quarter
TB - Dudley 35 pass from B.Johnson (Gramatica kick), 14:53. Drive: 5 plays, 66 yards, 2:30.
TB - McCardell 65 pass from B.Johnson (Gramatica kick), 7:34. Drive: 2 plays, 70 yards, :39.
TB - Quarles 25 interception return (Gramatica kick), :52.

Third Quarter
TB - Dilger 22 pass from B.Johnson (Gramatica kick), 10:46. Drive: 5 plays, 37 yards, 2:31.

Fourth Quarter
TB - Alstott 1 run (Gramatica kick), 3:08. Drive: 7 plays, 46 yards, 3:39.
A - 57,234.

REACTION
"We're nice right now. We've got two cats up front, me and Sapp, who are basically unstoppable. Yeah, we've got something special going on." —Simeon Rice

NUMBERS GAME
Tampa Bay had three touchdown passes of more than 20 yards for the first time since Oct. 31, 1993, in a 31-24 victory at Atlanta.

ROAD BLOWOUT
The largest margin of victory for the Bucs as a visiting team:

Points	Score	Home team	Date
35	35-0	Cincinnati	Dec. 27, 1998
28	35-7	Cincinnati	Sept. 29, 2002
25	25-0	Baltimore	Sept. 15, 2002
21	31-10	Detroit	Sept. 17, 2000
19	33-14	New Orleans	Dec. 11, 1977

NFC SOUTH STANDINGS

	W	L	T
Carolina	3	1	0
New Orleans	3	1	0
Tampa Bay	3	1	0
Atlanta	1	2	0

Game 4

BUCS 35, BENGALS 7

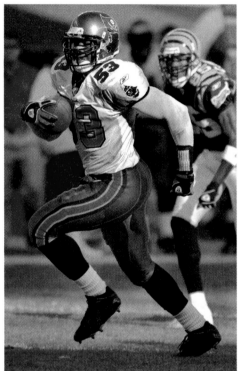

Quarles added to the rout, picking off a pass and sprinting 25 yards for a score with 52 seconds left in the first half.

McCardell was left alone when the Bengals bungled their coverage, sticking three defenders on Keyshawn Johnson.

drives as soon as we took the field. So we were determined not to let any of that happen today."

Until this victory, the Bucs had never shut out two opposing offenses in back-to-back road games.

By calling for an array of blitzes, the Bengals were leaving open the deep middle of the field, where the tight ends and an occasional receiver were left in single coverage against a safety.

The Bucs first tried to attack that area in their third offensive series, when Johnson threw deep but just beyond the grasp of a wide open Rickey Dudley, who was streaking alone down the numbers on the left side of the field.

One series later, after Cincinnati's Brian Simmons gave the Bengals a 7–0 lead with a 51-yard interception return, Brad Johnson connected with a lonesome Dudley on a similar pass play, this one resulting in a 35-yard touchdown.

"They were playing a single safety in the middle of the field and any time you get that, you are going to have some chances to get open," Dudley said. "The chance was there for me and we took advantage of it."

Those kinds of chances were still there later in the second quarter, when Keenan McCardell took off downfield after completing a simple curl pattern along the left sideline.

When three defenders converged on Keyshawn Johnson, who was running a hook pattern, McCardell was left alone. Despite being hit just as he released the ball, Brad Johnson connected with McCardell in stride on a 65-yard scoring play that was the longest the Bucs have had since Trent Dilfer connected with Reidel Anthony on a 79-yarder on November 15, 1998, against Jacksonville.

"Those types of things usually don't happen," said Brad Johnson, who threw for 277 yards and three touchdowns. But when the throws are downfield, we're going to take them. That's what we did."

Roy Cummings

Sapp and Anthony McFarland made Akili Smith's day very difficult. Sapp said last year's trip to Cincinnati stuck in his mind as the Bucs shut out another opponent's offense.

Keyshawn flew solo down the sideline on a 76-yard touchdown reception, the longest of his career. It put the Bucs ahead for good in the third quarter.

Game 5

Bucs 20, Falcons 6
October 6 at Atlanta

Can It Get Any Better?

The Bucs' defense sets the bar pretty high to begin with. Ever since Warren Sapp, Derrick Brooks and John Lynch came aboard, it always has.

And in the three games they played before facing the Falcons at the Georgia Dome, the Bucs thought their defensive effort finally reached those lofty standards.

That's why Brooks was a little stunned to hear Jon Gruden raise the bar on the defense during their team meeting the night before the game.

"He told us to go out and unleash something on this league that it's never seen before," Brooks said after the 20–6 victory. "I thought we'd done that already."

They had. In their previous three games, Bucs defenders had given up an average of 4.7 points per game while scoring a touchdown per game themselves.

Against the Falcons, the Bucs kept that run alive. The defense kept a road opponent out of the end zone for the third consecutive game and scored a touchdown for the fourth game in a row.

Atlanta, with elusive quarterback Michael Vick and able runners like T. J. Duckett and Warrick Dunn, never had a

---

First Quarter
Atl - FG Feely 34, 7:05. Drive: 6 plays, 16 yards, 3:14.

Second Quarter
TB - FG Gramatica 23, 8:03. Drive: 14 plays, 56 yards, 6:39.

Third Quarter
Atl - FG Feely 32, 6:18. Drive: 6 plays, 43 yards, 2:56.
TB - K.Johnson 76 pass from B.Johnson (Gramatica kick), 4:32.

Fourth Quarter
TB - FG Gramatica 22, 6:31. Drive: 10 plays, 49 yards, 4:54.
TB - Brooks 15 interception return (Gramatica kick), 6:14
A - 68,936.

REACTION
"There's nothing wrong with shooting for the moon. If you miss, you wind up deep in the stars. That's where we are. We're on it right now." —Warren Sapp

NUMBERS GAME
By beating Atlanta, the Bucs tied the team record for consecutive road victories with three. The team has won three straight on the road four other times, most recently from November 11 to December 2, 2001 (Detroit, St. Louis, Cincinnati).

FALCONS PLUCKED
The Bucs put constant pressure on Falcons quarterbacks, never gave up a big play, made their own big plays and didn't allow a touchdown. A look at their defensive domination in the victory at Atlanta:

Interceptions: **4**
Sacks: **4**
Plays over 20 yards: **0**
Touchdowns allowed: **0**
Touchdowns scored: **1**
Third downs converted by Atlanta: **3-14** (21 percent)
Yards allowed per rush attempt: **3.2**
Yards allowed per pass attempt: **4.6**

NFC SOUTH STANDINGS

	W	L	T
New Orleans	4	1	0
Tampa Bay	4	1	0
Carolina	3	2	0
Atlanta	1	3	0

Within the photo/newspaper clipping:

BUCS BONUS
MONDAY, OCTOBER 7, 2002 · THE TAMPA TRIBUNE · TBO.com

Bucs Raise The Bar

Key Gruden Slowly Building Some Trust

BUCS 20, FALCONS 6

play more than 20 yards and finished with 243 net yards.

Vick was never a factor. Simeon Rice's sack took Vick out of the game with a shoulder injury, Doug Johnson replaced him and the Falcons' fate was all but decided.

"Once we got Vick out of the game, we could go back to our old style of playing again, where we're going after the passer and rushing straight at him," Sapp said. "You can't do that with Vick in there; he's too dangerous. But after he was out, it was just shooting arrows. [Johnson] ain't going to beat us."

In their last four games, the Bucs allowed a total of just 27 points. That's the stingiest four-game stretch in team history, and during that span the defense has outscored opposing offenses 30–20.

Brooks has done most of the scoring. He had another touchdown against Atlanta, taking a lateral from Sapp and running it in from the Falcons' 15 after Sapp had intercepted Johnson.

"I heard 'Doom,' and I knew Brooks was two yards back," Sapp said, "so I just flipped it to him."

"Doom." That's what Brooks calls Sapp, his training-camp roommate. It's a nickname. It became a signal, one that Sapp

With help from his training-camp roommate, Brooks again found the end zone. It was the defense's fourth interception return for a touchdown.

Michael Vick was never a factor. The Falcons' star was held to 37 yards passing and 1 yard rushing before Rice knocked him out of the game.

interpreted to mean that Brooks was coming up from behind and was in position to make a play.

The only pitch that damaged the Falcons more was made by Brad Johnson. With the Bucs trailing 6–3 late in the third quarter, he connected with Keyshawn Johnson on a 76-yard touchdown pass that gave the Bucs a lead they would never lose.

Roy Cummings

Doug Johnson didn't fare much better than Vick, as Rice, Greg Spires and other Bucs defenders were relentless in the second half.

After talking with Gruden about his role, Alstott was sucking wind and loving it against the Browns. He saw "huge holes" in the Cleveland defense en route to a 126-yard game.

Game 6

Bucs 17, Browns 3
October 13 at Tampa

Back on Track

It's hard to keep Mike Alstott down. Just ask the Browns, who needed two or three defenders—and sometimes the entire defense—to tackle Tampa Bay's "A-Train."

Adversity wasn't going to keep Alstott down either. Relegated to the sideline for most of the season, Alstott found his way back onto the field and took advantage of it.

For the seventh time in his seven-year career, Alstott passed the 100-yard rushing mark when he ran for a game-high 126 yards on 17 carries and two touchdowns against Cleveland, sealing a 17–3 victory.

Since 1997, the Bucs are 26–5 when Alstott scores a touchdown.

In his five previous games, Alstott posted only 82 yards on 33 carries and two touchdowns. Newcomer Michael Pittman had been getting the bulk of the carries.

Against the Browns, there were times when Alstott was doubled over trying to catch his breath. "I loved it," Alstott said. "I loved sucking wind out there. I haven't felt like that in a long time. Let's do it every week."

Alstott met with coach Jon Gruden earlier in the week, not to beg for the ball, but to get a clear understanding of his job with the team.

GAME SUMMARY

Bucs	7	3	0	7 -	17
Browns	0	0	0	3 -	3

First Quarter

TB - Alstott 1 run (Gramatica kick), 9:01. Drive: 5 plays, 80 yards, 2:57.

Second Quarter

TB - FG Gramatica 33, 2:42. Drive: 6 plays, 12 yards, 2:17.

Fourth Quarter

TB - Alstott 17 run (Gramatica kick), 14:51. Drive: 5 plays, 55 yards, 2:19.
CL - FG Dawson 55, 11:45. Drive: 9 plays, 42 yards, 3:06.
A - 65,625

REACTION

"We knew the only way they were going to move the ball on us was if they got some penalties. I mean, we talk about being dominant around here every week. That's what we're looking to do." —John Lynch

NUMBERS GAME

For the third time this season, the Bucs' defense held opponents to less than 200 total yards. It also extended to 12 the number of quarters the unit has held opposing offenses without a touchdown.

ALSTOTT'S BEST

Mike Alstott never had fewer carries in a 100-yard effort than the 17 he had against Cleveland. Here are his top rushing performances:

Date	Att-Yds.	Opponent
Sept. 26, 1999	25-131	Broncos
Oct. 28, 2001	28-129	Vikings
Nov. 1, 1998	19-128	Vikings
Oct. 13, 2002	17-126	Browns
Nov. 17, 1999	25-117	at Saints
Sept. 20, 1998	20-103	Bears
Dec. 23, 2001	24-101	Saints

NFC SOUTH STANDINGS

	W	L	T
New Orleans	5	1	0
Tampa Bay	5	1	0
Carolina	3	3	0
Atlanta	2	3	0

When the running room closed down, the A-Train was bouncing off Browns. Alstott scored twice, and his running wore down the visitors in the Tampa heat.

"I just talked with him to see how he felt I was doing, what he saw my role as," Alstott said. "We just had a normal conversation . . . I just asked him, 'What do you see me as?' and 'How do you see me in your offense?' We just talked. I didn't expect to get the ball like this. I just wanted to be on the field with my teammates and be a part of something and make some plays."

By putting just seven defenders near the line of scrimmage, the Browns challenged the Bucs to run. The Bucs met the challenge, running for 186 total yards.

Sapp sacked Cleveland's Tim Couch twice as the Browns could muster only a 50-yard field goal.

Dexter Jackson kept Jamal White and the Browns' offense scoreless as the Bucs' defense completed a 12-quarter skunking over the past three games.

"Nothing but huge holes. That's all my eyes could see," Alstott said. "Straight ahead, cutbacks, wherever I looked. And I was looking hard. It was a great feeling. That offensive line would not stop."

As the day wore on, Cleveland flat wore out. By the fourth quarter, the Browns' defense was running on empty and with little purpose. About the only thing at Raymond James Stadium that wasn't hot that day was Cleveland's defensive pursuit.

"We wore them down," said Pittman, who also ran for 53 yards. "They were very tired. You could tell in the fourth quarter they were ready to give up. One time I saw a guy kick the ball just so he could stop the clock again after the official set it up. That's what you want in the fourth quarter. You want your offense to dominate in the running game. I think we did that."

Katherine Smith, Mick Elliott

Al Harris made sure a victory in Philadelphia remained out of reach for Keyshawn and the Bucs.

Game 7

Eagles 20, **Bucs 10**
October 20 at Philadelphia

The Hex Continues

Bucs safety Dexter Jackson sat inside his Veterans Stadium dressing stall late after the game, shaking his head and pondering the death grip the Eagles had applied to his team's throat.

"I don't know what more we can do," Jackson said after Tampa Bay's fourth consecutive loss to the Eagles. "I guess we just can't let 'em score on us."

The Bucs' offense produced one field goal and no touchdowns. It has been 13 quarters since the Bucs scored an offensive touchdown in Philadelphia.

And the team lost quarterback Brad Johnson to a rib injury. Backup Rob Johnson finished the game.

When Todd Pinkston beat Jackson on a 42-yard fly pattern in the second quarter, it was the first time in 13 quarters that Tampa Bay's defense had given up a touchdown. That TD also was the first surrendered by the Bucs' defense on the road this year and gave Philadelphia a 10–7 halftime lead.

Before that, the Bucs had a 7–3 lead and momentum after Derrick Brooks picked up a Donovan McNabb fumble and returned it 11 yards for his fourth touchdown of the year.

The momentum actually increased when Brian Kelly

GAME SUMMARY

Bucs	7	0	3	0 -	10
Eagles	3	7	3	7 -	20

First Quarter

P - FG Akers 30, 10:29. Drive: 4 plays, 2 yards, 1:20

TB - Brooks 11 fumble return (Gramatica kick), 5:39.

Second Quarter

P - Pinkston 42 pass from McNabb (Akers kick), 2:29. Drive: 2 plays, 45 yards, 0:41.

Third Quarter

P - FG Akers 35, 6:22. Drive: 11 plays, 45 yards, 4:56.

TB - FG Gramatica 48, 2:39. Drive: 9 plays, 50 yards, 3:43.

Fourth Quarter

P - McNabb 1 run (Akers kick), 8:18. Drive: 10 plays, 42 yards, 5:37.

A - 65,523.

REACTION

"I'm sure we don't worry them. I think they probably respect the individual players, but can't blame them for not respecting the entire defense. If that bothers us, it's up to us to do something about it." —John Lynch on the Eagles

NUMBERS GAME

Derrick Brooks, who returned a fumble for a touchdown against the Eagles, became the first NFL player with four defensive scores since Eric Allen in 1993. The NFL record is five, by Ken Houston in 1971.

DOG DAYS AT THE VET

Going into this game, the Bucs' offense last scored a touchdown in Philadelphia during a 19-5 win on September 19, 1999. Here are the three games since that victory:

Date	Result	Comment
Dec. 31, 2000	Eagles 21, Bucs 3	Bucs rush for 50 yards.
Jan. 12, 2002	Eagles 31, Bucs 9	Four Bucs turnovers.
Oct. 20, 2002	Eagles 20, Bucs 10	Bucs 3-for-13 on third downs.

NFC SOUTH STANDINGS

	W	L	T
New Orleans	6	1	0
Tampa Bay	5	2	0
Atlanta	3	3	0
Carolina	3	4	0

Brooks scored again, running 11 yards with a Donovan McNabb fumble and giving the Bucs early hope.

Pittman had nowhere to run as the Bucs managed only 207 yards of total offense.

picked off a McNabb pass on the Eagles' next play from scrimmage. But the Bucs failed to capitalize.

The Eagles used an array of blitzes, often sending more players after the quarterback than the Bucs had players to protect him.

"They just whupped us," center Jeff Christy said. "I mean, they made it look at times like we didn't know what we were doing out there."

Stopping return man Brian Mitchell was a problem for the Bucs as well. Mitchell, who averaged 12.2 yards per punt return and 27.7 yards per kick return, regularly set up the Eagles with good field position.

Despite Mitchell's success, the Bucs' defense did not let Philadelphia take full advantage of the opportunities he presented. And though Alstott's fumble gave them the ball at the Tampa Bay 14, the Eagles settled for a field goal.

McNabb also was shut down for much of the game. He completed 12 of 25 passes for 127 yards and ran six times for 4 yards.

Simeon Rice, who forced the McNabb fumble, was disappointed, but not discouraged.

"This is only the beginning for us," he said. "We've got charisma and we've got character, and we were tested today. We played hard and I expect to see the Eagles again this year. We'll be ready."

Roy Cummings

Rice picked up a sack, and the Bucs kept McNabb in check, but the Eagles' quarterback still ran for a touchdown and passed for another.

Gramatica was automatica against the Panthers, booting four field goals. A 53-yarder, his second from beyond 50 yards, tied the game in the fourth quarter.

Game 8

Bucs 12, Panthers 9
October 27 at Charlotte

Martin to the Rescue

There's always a way. Even when you're down to your third quarterback, your fifth wide receiver and the last option in your playbook.

The key is to discover it, and that's what Jon Gruden had been encouraging the Bucs to do: find a way to succeed; find a way to win.

He found what he was looking for by turning to his kicker.

Martin Gramatica broke out of a 2-for-5 slump and guided the Bucs to a 12–9 victory against Carolina by turning in a 4-for-4 effort that transcended football in the eyes of some.

"Martin is our Barry Bonds,"

John Lynch said. "If we get the ball down for him, get it set and block some people, he's going to hit some three-run homers and do some damage."

Gramatica did most of his damage in the fourth quarter, erasing a 9–3 deficit by going deep with field goals of 52, 53 and 47 yards, the second of which was his longest of the season.

The last kick, with five seconds remaining, allowed the Bucs to jump into a tie with New Orleans for first place in the NFC South.

"I looked at Gramatica and said, 'Can you make this?' " Gruden said. "There was no doubt in my mind he was going to make the kick."

BUCS BONUS
KICK SAVE

The Bucs Didn't Invent Winning Ugly. But They're Starting To Perfect It

First Quarter
TB - FG Gramatica 32, 4:57. Drive: 8 plays, 39 yards, 4:50.

Second Quarter
C - FG Graham 20, 10:52. Drive: 4 plays, 9 yards, 1:30.

Third Quarter
C - FG Graham 47, 8:44. Drive: 12 plays, 44 yards, 6:16.
C - FG Graham 39, 1:36. Drive: 10 plays, 34 yards, 5:22.

Fourth Quarter
TB - FG Gramatica 52, 10:05. Drive: 9 plays, 30 yards, 3:00.
TB - FG Gramatica 53, 1:55. Drive: 4 plays, 7 yards, 1:06.
TB - FG Gramatica 47, 0:05. Drive: 8 plays, 44 yards, 1:10.
A - 63,354

REACTION
"If we get the ball down for him, get it set and block some people, he's going to hit some three-run homers and do some damage." —John Lynch

NUMBERS GAME
Carolina's Randy Fasani, with five completions and three interceptions, finished with a quarterback rating of 0.0.

NO TOUCHDOWN NEEDED
Bucs victories in which they did not score a touchdown:

Score	Opponent	Date
15-0	at Chicago	Dec. 29, 2002
12-9	at Carolina	Oct. 27, 2002
6-3	Chicago	Oct. 24, 1999
3-0	Kansas City	Dec. 16, 1979

NFC SOUTH STANDINGS

	W	L	T
New Orleans	6	2	0
Tampa Bay	6	2	0
Atlanta	4	3	0
Carolina	3	5	0

"It was 53 yards," recalled Gramatica, "and I said I could give it a shot. Thank God I made it. If I miss it, he won't believe me next time."

Rob Johnson, who was sacked six times, started in place of Brad Johnson and completed 22 of 33 passes under constant pressure. Although he did cough up a fumble and throw an interception, his play drew praise from his coach.

"He kept our team moving and won as a starter," Gruden said.

The same could not be said of Carolina's Randy Fasani. A rookie making his first NFL start, Fasani did not complete his first pass until 5:35 remained in what proved to be a record-setting first half for the Bucs defense. By holding Carolina to 15 total yards, including minus-4 passing, the Bucs set two single-half team records during the first 30 minutes, which ended with a 3–3 tie.

The Panthers came out stronger offensively in the second half and built a 9–3 edge. They intercepted Johnson to end one drive and forced the Bucs to go three and out on another. But they

The Panthers were physical, pressuring backup Rob Johnson into some costly mistakes. But he made the plays necessary to put Gramatica in field-goal range.

Randy Fasani got a rude welcome in his first NFL start. Sapp and Co. held the rookie to minus-four yards passing in the first half.

couldn't shut down Gramatica.

After his 52-yard field goal made it a 9–6 game, he tied it by hitting the 53-yarder set up when Carolina punt returner Steve Smith fumbled at his own 42-yard line.

The Bucs then mounted their game-winning drive, which succeeded thanks primarily to the clutch play of reserves such as quarterback Shawn King, receiver Reggie Barlow and long snapper Ryan Benjamin.

Barlow, who had been inactive for each of the Bucs' first six games, caught a key six-yard pass early in the drive.

Then, after Johnson took a hit at the end of a nine-yard third-down run that kept him from continuing, King rushed into the game to hit Karl Williams with a seven-yard pass that put the Bucs into field-goal range.

Finally, Benjamin fired a bullet back to Tom Tupa, the holder, despite suffering from a hamstring strain that made it nearly impossible for him to bend over. All that remained was for Gramatica to send the ball through the uprights, which he did.

"Everybody would like to be the Raiders and score a lot of touchdowns," Johnson said. "But we're finding ways to win and that's what's important."

Roy Cummings

Lamar Smith covers up before Rice and Chartric Darby make contact. The Bucs' defense allowed only 15 yards in the first 30 minutes.

Sapp was there to congratulate Gramatica after the fourth kick won the game and moved the Bucs into a first-place tie with the Saints.

There's always a place on a roster for quarterbacks who play smart, well and occasionally hurt. That's Brad Johnson, who threw a career-high 5 touchdown passes against Minnesota.

Bucs 38, Vikings 24
November 3 at Tampa

Mr. Consistent

It was not lost on Brad Johnson - nothing ever is - that his career-high five touchdown passes came against the Minnesota Vikings, his first NFL team, where his journey began 10 years ago.

"I had a lot of hay in my hair then," Johnson said.

Everywhere he has gone in this league, a crowd has gathered to say there was somebody better on the farm.

It was no different here. Rob Johnson. Shaun King. Always the talk. Brad Johnson has heard it often.

"I'm not a flashy guy," he said. "I'm going to be consistent. You're not going to see a lot of highlight films of me on TV. You're not going to see me dance, or catch a lot of one-liners from me. I'm going to be as consistent as you can be."

He is forever matched against a younger, sexier talent, the new and improved NFL quarterback. Against Minnesota, it was Daunte Culpepper -- bigger, stronger and faster.

But there always will be a place for Brad Johnsons on football rosters. A place for playing hurt, smart and well.

A week ago, Johnson felt a knife in his side each time he took a breath. It still hurt, but not as much. Johnson's decision came from the heart beneath those ribs.

"You can't miss days like this."

GAME SUMMARY

Bucs	14	10	7	7 -	38
Vikings	0	10	7	7 -	24

First Quarter

TB - K. Williams 15 pass from B. Johnson (Gramatica kick), 13:12. Drive: 3 plays, 21 yards, 1:41.

TB - Dudley 2 pass from B. Johnson (Gramatica kick), 1:03. Drive: 12 plays, 86 yards, 6:09.

Second Quarter

TB - FG Gramatica 36, 12:16. Drive: 6 plays, 30 yards, 2:44.

TB - K. Johnson 2 pass from B. Johnson (Gramatica kick), 7:16. Drive: 5 plays, 184 yards, 1:52.

M - Bennett 85 run (Anderson kick), 6:49. Drive: 1 play, 75 yards, 0:27.

M - FG Anderson 26, 0:00. Drive: 8 plays, 61 yards, 2:02.

Third Quarter

TB - K. Johnson 19 pass from B. Johnson. (Gramatica kick), 5:10. Drive: 6 plays, 82 yards, 3:59.

M - M. Williams 1 run (Anderson kick), 2:08. Drive: 6 plays, 64 yards, 3:02.

Fourth Quarter

TB - Alstott 1 pass from B. Johnson (Gramatica kick), 13:34. Drive: 6 plays, 46 yards, 3:17.

M - M. Williams 1 run (Anderson kick), 4:40. Drive: 12 plays, 88 yards, 5:43.

A - 65,667

REACTION

"I can go all season long without catching a pass. As long as we win, I'm doing something in our offense."
— Keyshawn Johnson

NUMBERS GAME

It was the first game in five years the Bucs won while allowing a 100-yard rusher. Minnesota's Michael Bennett ran for 114. The Bucs had lost 12 straight against 100-yard rushers.

NFC SOUTH STANDINGS

	W	L	T
Tampa Bay	7	2	0
New Orleans	6	2	0
Atlanta	5	3	0
Carolina	3	5	0

Aaron Stecker's 59-yard sprint set up a touchdown that gave the Bucs a 24-0 lead. The play gave the Bucs' nearly half of their rushing yards.

Nick Davis fumbled the opening kickoff and Jermaine Phillips recovered. The Bucs made it 7-0 three plays later.

He wore his usual padding, nothing extra over the rib he cracked in Philadelphia, where he took another beating. He sucked it up and breathed life into an offense riddled with injuries and doubt.

Never mind that it came against the Minnesota defense. The Bucs needed this. And when he was needed, when we wondered what he would do, Brad Johnson played his best game as a Buc.

His numbers sparkled: 24 of 31 passing, 313 yards, five TDs, no interceptions. A season-high 446 yards of total offense. Johnson's favorite numbers were 7 and 2 -- his team's record.

Johnson's teammates always get around to his toughness. "That's why they call him "The Bull,' " Bucs offensive lineman Todd Washington said. "Pain or no pain, cracked ribs or no cracked ribs, he's going to come out and give everything he's got. We rally around that."

The Bucs' offensive line didn't let anyone near those ribs. Johnson concentrated on his own targets, including his favorite one.

Johnson & Johnson. Wasn't this how it was always supposed to be? Brad getting time and pinpointing it to Keyshawn, who grabs everything.

They hooked up nine times for 133 yards. Keyshawn scored two touchdowns.

Before the game, Keyshawn was talking with someone when the someone blurted out the standard line: Brad Johnson wasn't good enough.

"Let me tell you something," Keyshawn said. "You give that man time and that dude's going to dice somebody up."

Brad Johnson might not be the best at anything in this league. He's not good enough to overcome bad protection. His deep ball remains suspect.

Can he win a game all by himself? No.

Is he a winner? Yes.

Give him time and he will thread a needle. He will get you home. He won't cost you the game, and he might just win one.

His next bad game will start the next quarterback controversy. But there always will be a place for Brad Johnsons in this league.

Want to know why? Simply ask them if they're ready to go. If they are, and sometimes even if they aren't, they'll be consistent. They'll say the same thing every time.

You can't miss days like this.

Martin Fennelly

Sure, the offense could be "friendlier," in the eyes of the beholder. But an 8-2 record warranted no explanations from Keyshawn and his teammates.

Bucs 23, Panthers 10
November 18 at Tampa

No Apology Needed

Jon Gruden would like to say he's sorry. He'd like to say he's sorry from the bottom of his heart, which rested, along with his team, atop the NFC South and tied atop the NFL leaderboard after defeating Carolina a second time. The Bucs' head coach would like to beg for your forgiveness.

We said he'd *like* to.

Chucky don't beg.

"What am I supposed to do," Gruden said, "apologize for being 8–2?"

The victory gave the Bucs the best record in football, along with the Green Bay Packers, Tampa Bay's next opponent.

After Green Bay, the Bucs get New Orleans and Atlanta. A few more wins and they would be awash in playoff tiebreakers. You couldn't deny their increasingly enviable position. Nor could they, especially veterans who know Buc history. John Lynch alluded to Sam Wyche when considering the state of the franchise.

"We've had 5-dash-2, but never 8-dash-2."

Warren Sapp had never been to the land of 8–2 as a professional. Strange feeling. Good feeling. For the record, he felt that the complaints about how the Bucs have looked getting to this record sound like a broken record.

First Quarter

C - S.Smith 20 pass from Peete (Graham kick), 6:06. Drive: 9 plays, 70 yards, 5:45.

Second Quarter

TB - K.Johnson 1 pass from B.Johnson (Gramatica kick), 9:27. Drive: 13 plays, 86 yards, 6:23.
C - FG Graham 42, 6:25. Drive: 4 plays, 4 yards, 1:16.
TB - FG Gramatica 20, 3:00. Drive: 8 plays, 59 yards, 3:25.

Third Quarter

TB - McCardell 22 pass from B.Johnson (Gramatica kick), 1:28. Drive: 2 plays, 19 yards, 0:52.

Fourth Quarter

TB - FG Gramatica 32, 8:03. Drive: 12 plays, 54 yards, 6:38.
TB - FG Gramatica 41, 3:57. Drive: 7 plays, 8 yards, 3:52.
A - 65,527

REACTION

"In a lot of stadiums, people leave their seats and go get a Coke when the defense is on the field. I don't think that happens here. I think that's when it gets loudest. And we like that." —John Lynch

NUMBERS GAME

In the second half, the Bucs' defense allowed only 93 yards total offense, forced three turnovers and notched three sacks, two by Simeon Rice.

LIVING UP TO NUMBER ONE

Here's how Carolina fared on its first six possessions of the second half against the NFL's top-rated defense:

Drive began	Plays	Yards	1st Downs	Result
Panthers 36	3	4	0	Punt
Panthers 46	3	9	0	Punt
Panthers 43	2	0	0	Fumble
Panthers 15	3	2	0	Interception
Panthers 30	3	9	0	Punt
Panthers 27	1	0	0	Interception

NFC SOUTH STANDINGS

	W	L	T
Tampa Bay	8	2	0
New Orleans	7	3	0
Atlanta	6	3	1
Carolina	3	6	0

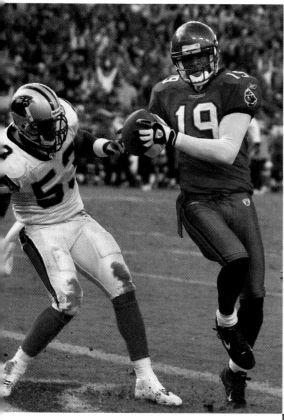

"There's a row that says wins and a row that says losses, and they just rack 'em," Sapp said. "They don't say you beat [Carolina] by 3 the last time or by 13 this time. They just rack 'em. They say, "Where you at?'"

The man who caught the winning points agreed. Keenan McCardell's catch of a Brad Johnson floater had an 8-dash-2 of hilarity. McCardell grabbed the ball inside the 10 and turned to make a move, break a tackle, take a hit, something.

But there was no one there. Panthers cornerback Terry Cousin had turned out as McCardell turned in for the post. McCardell could have rolled the ball into the end zone with his nose.

To snooty skeptics, that sums up Buc success. Never mind the monster defense or that parts of the offense are showing improvement. They are on top because no one bothers stopping them. The critics croon.

McCardell just smiles. In 1999, he played for a Jacksonville Jaguars team that went 14–2, and along the way he heard the things he hears now.

"We were running under the radar," McCardell said. "I don't mind if we keep running under the radar here. That's cool. We'll just keep winning. We don't need glitz or glory."

Keyshawn contributed his fourth TD catch of the season, along with 74 yards on seven catches.

McCardell waited for a hit that never came, then dashed 22 yards to keep the Bucs flying under the radar.

Keyshawn Johnson, who has never minded glitz or glory, still dug what Keenan said. Keyshawn also scored, though he made his points on fourth-and-goal to get the Bucs into this game. It was his fourth score of the year.

"We can continue to thrash people the way we do," Keyshawn said. "I'm slow. I'm no good. Brad is over the hill. His arm isn't strong enough. Warren Sapp talks too much. Keenan McCardell is too old. We don't have no running game. I'll continue to live with that at 8–2 and move on to 9–2."

It will take more than this defense, which was ridiculously good when it counted against Carolina. It will take more. The head coach knows that, too. But Gruden sounded more sick than tired of having to examine victories as if they were losses.

"We would like to be, how shall I say, friendlier to your eyes in terms of all our plays in the game. Sure," says Gruden. "But I'm proud of this team. . . . We're finding ways to win in a league where that's really pretty hard."

For the record, Gruden turned to team physician Joe Diaco, who has been with the Bucs since shortly after the knee was invented.

"Doc, you ever been 8–2?" Gruden asked.

"Nope," Diaco said.

By God, rack it up.

Martin Fennelly

Gramatica racked up another three field goals against Carolina. The final kick, from 41 yards, came after a John Lynch interception, below.

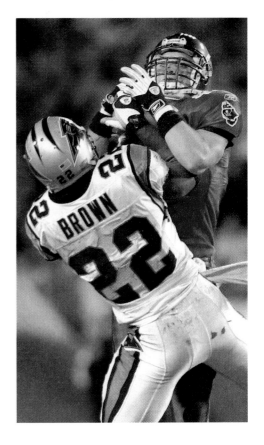

After the referee overturned the ruling on the field, Jurevicius got his touchdown … and a souvenir.

Bucs 21, Packers 7
November 24 at Tampa

The Perfect Pass

The throw was long and true. It was perfectly delivered, under some pressure.

In time, the Bucs might consider it the most important toss of their season. After all, it allowed them to surge ahead of the Packers and set up a 21–7 victory. Tampa Bay took control of homefield advantage in the NFC playoffs and might have cleared a nice path to Super Bowl XXXVII.

That's a pretty crucial pass.

But you'll never find it on Tampa Bay's 2002 highlight film.

Because this wasn't even a football. It was a red beanbag.

Here was Tampa Bay's game-winning reversal of fortune.

The Bucs, trailing Green Bay 7–6 in the third quarter, faced second-and-goal from the Packers' 4-yard line. Brad Johnson appeared to hit Joe Jurevicius near the end zone sideline for a go-ahead touchdown, with tight coverage from Packers' cornerback Tyrone Williams, but the trailing official ruled no catch. Out of bounds.

Jon Gruden didn't flinch, sending in a third-down play. He thought it was over. When press-box staffers finally saw the replay TV feed, it seemed clear that Jurevicius had possession and got both feet in bounds. Gruden got that word when the play clock approached 10

GAME SUMMARY

Bucs	0	3	11	7	- 21
Packers	7	0	0	0	- 7

First Quarter
GB - Driver 4 pass from Favre (Longwell kick), 5:44. Drive: 6 plays, 30 yards, 2:57.

Second Quarter
TB - FG Gramatica 38, 0:00. Drive: 3 plays, 39 yards, 0:23.

Third Quarter
TB - Jurevicius 4 pass from B.Johnson (K.Johnson pass from B. Johnson), 5:00. Drive: 4 plays, 18 yards,

Fourth Quarter
TB - Dilger 3 pass from B.Johnson (Gramatica kick), 7:24. Drive: 3 plays, 2 yards, 1:18.
A - 65,672

REACTION
"What we did was put the pedal to the metal and lap Green Bay. Now we'll go to New Orleans and see if we can lap them. Believe me, we realize what's ahead of us." —Warren Sapp

NUMBERS GAME
With two interceptions against the Packers, Brian Kelly moved into the NFL lead with six. He finished the season as the league's co-leader with eight. His first pick set up Joe Jurevicius' go-ahead touchdown catch. His second, late in the fourth quarter, stopped a potential Packers scoring drive.

CAN'T STAND THE HEAT
Brett Favre's five games at Raymond James Stadium:

Date	Comp.	Att.	Yds.	TD	Int.
Dec. 7, 1998	29	41	262	2	0
Dec. 26, 1999	25	48	234	1	2
Nov. 12, 2000*	14	25	117	0	0
Oct. 7, 2001	20	35	258	1	3
Nov. 24, 2002	20	38	196	1	4

* Favre was knocked out of the game by a Warren Sapp sack in the third quarter.

NFC SOUTH STANDINGS

	W	L	T
Tampa Bay	9	2	0
Atlanta	7	3	1
New Orleans	7	4	0
Carolina	3	8	0

Rice reacquainted Brett Favre with the turf at Raymond James Stadium. Rice had two sacks for the fourth straight game.

seconds. He frantically pressed his replay-challenge button. Somehow, officials weren't getting the signal.

Enter the beanbag.

Made possible, of course, by the perfectly executed toe-drag.

When the replay was shown on Raymond James Stadium's video board, the fans went ballistic. Jurevicius was in! Tampa Bay's sideline erupted with emotion. "Challenge! Challenge! Challenge! We were all screaming. That was a touchdown!" Dexter Jackson said.

But Gruden's replay-challenge button wasn't working. The window was closing. That's when Gruden implored his personal assistant, Mark Arteaga, to get the officials' attention. Throw the beanbag!

Initially, Arteaga struggled to grab it.

Throw it!

"If he didn't get [the beanbag] out of his pocket, we were going to throw him on the field," Gruden said.

Arteaga was clutch with an Olympic-like toss that shattered all Ray-Jay beanbag records. The replay challenge was on. Bucs players never had a doubt.

There was even some physical evidence . . . a telltale clump of grass, uprooted by Jurevicius' dragging foot.

Here's how referee Johnny Grier described the decision:

"After reviewing the play, the receiver gained control of the ball in the air. His right foot hit down. He dotted the "i" with the left foot, maintained possession when he hit the ground. We have a touchdown."

A critical reversal of fortune . . . thanks to the beanbag and that perfectly executed toe-drag.

Each day at practice, Jurevicius works on over the shoulder receptions near the sideline. The key: keeping both feet in bounds. It's monotonous repetition. It would be easy to slack off. But receivers coach Richard Mann won't permit that.

"He's a stickler for that toe-drag technique," Jurevicius said. "If you mess it up on the practice field, the film doesn't lie. It has to be perfect. It has to be in your mind on every single catch."

"Upon further review," Gruden said, "I truly thought it was one of the great toe-drags I had ever seen. Plus, Jurevicius has big feet. That makes for an easy review."

"Joe had a little pirouette move," Bucs defensive end Simeon Rice said. "Very sweet. Very swan-like. Matter of fact, very Lynn Swann-like."

Instead of a postgame celebration, Sapp found a confrontation with Mike Sherman. The Packers' coach was upset after Sapp's legal block injured Green Bay's Chad Clifton.

Jurevicius said he had one thought when seeing the replay—"Touchdown"—but waited until it was official. He raced after the ball, which had been placed back at the line of scrimmage, and spiked it in the end zone. Then he quickly retrieved it for a souvenir sports room that he's planning. "When something memorable happens, I want to keep the ball," Jurevicius said. "And this is one I'll always remember."

The Bucs will remember it, too.

"I thought Mark Arteaga was one of the great acquisitions we made in the off-season, and this throw does nothing but confirm that," Gruden said. "There's a thin line in this league. When the play is there, you need to make it."

By any means possible.

With a beanbag and a toe-drag, if that's what it takes.

Joey Johnson

Pittman ran for 17 yards during the game, an indicator of Tampa Bay's offensive woes.

Game 12

Saints 23, **Bucs** 20

December 1 at New Orleans

A Victim of Desperation

N obody would speak about it. Nobody would admit it.

The Bucs brought more than The Rock—their tangible, Jon Gruden–led inspiration for chiseled determination— to the Louisiana Superdome.

They also brought The Cushion.

Breathing room can be a dangerous thing. The Bucs were feeling good about things. Maybe too good. They had a four-game winning streak. They had beaten the Packers before a delirious home crowd. They had the NFL's best record.

For one of the few times in franchise history, they seemed in control of everything.

Everything!

My goodness, people were planning Super Bowl trips, a look-ahead prospect that made Gruden smirk. But you couldn't deny the feeling. The Bucs had big, big things ahead.

As it turned out, the Bucs weren't in control of much at all.

Except this: December was going to be one wild month.

They actually had plenty to fear, including a force that can't be underestimated in today's NFL.

Desperation.

New Orleans desperation.

If you're looking for a bottom line, that's why the New

GAME SUMMARY

Bucs	2	7	3	8	- 20
Saints	0	6	14	3	- 23

First Quarter

TB - Safety, fumble out of end zone, 3:17.

Second Quarter

NO - McCallister 6 run (two pt. conversion failed), 10:02. Drive: 10 plays, 80 yards, 5:12.

TB - Alstott 44 pass from B. Johnson (Gramatica kick), 6:51. Drive: 6 plays, 90 yards, 3:11.

Third Quarter

NO - J. Reed 3 pass from A. Brooks (Carney kick), 12:56. Drive: 6 plays, 54 yards, 2:04.

NO - Horn 14 pass from A. Brooks (Carney kick), 9:00. Drive: 3 plays, 20 yards, 1:31.

TB - FG Gramatica 51, 5:04. Drive: 9 plays, 39 yards, 3:56.

Fourth Quarter

NO - FG Carney 48, 9:47. Drive: 4 plays, 3 yards, 1:35.

TB - McCardell 2 pass from B. Johnson (K. Johnson pass from B. Johnson), 2:49. Drive: 17 plays, 84 yards, 6:58.

A - 68,226

TWO-TIMER

Simeon Rice set an NFL record against the Saints by becoming the first player with five consecutive games with two-plus sacks. Here's a sack-by-sack look at the streak:

DATE	OPPONENT	QUARTERBACK	YARDAGE
Oct. 27	at Carolina	Randy Fasani	-6 yards*
Oct. 27	at Carolina	Randy Fasani	-8 yards
Nov. 3	vs. Minnesota	Daunte Culpepper	-5 yards*
Nov. 3	vs. Minnesota	Daunte Culpepper	-5 yards
Nov. 17	vs. Carolina	Rodney Peete	-7 yards*
Nov. 17	vs. Carolina	Rodney Peete	-13 yards
Nov. 24	vs. Green Bay	Brett Favre	-6 yards
Nov. 24	vs. Green Bay	Brett Favre	-11 yards
Dec. 1	at New Orleans	Aaron Brooks	-1 yard
Dec. 1	at New Orleans	Aaron Brooks	-14 yards
Dec. 1	at New Orleans	Aaron Brooks	-10 yards*

*-Forced fumble on sack. **-Shared sack with Anthony McFarland.

NFC SOUTH STANDINGS

	W	L	T
Tampa Bay	9	3	0
Atlanta	8	3	1
New Orleans	8	4	0
Carolina	4	8	0

SAINTS 23, BUCS 20

Orleans Saints beat the Bucs 23–20. One more loss and the Saints could forget winning the division title. One more loss and they were fighting just to secure their No. 6–seeded playoff spot.

The Saints, who would've been ruined as division hopefuls, moved to a game back. More importantly, they swept the series with the Bucs. If the Saints and Bucs had finished in a tie for the NFC South title, the Saints would have been champions.

The Bucs would have been wild cards hitting the playoff road . . . again.

There's this little nugget as well. After that weekend, the Bucs, Packers and Eagles shared the NFC's best record. The Eagles controlled home-field advantage throughout the playoffs.

The Eagles. Just what you didn't want to hear.

The Bucs got a little feisty toward the end, driving 84 yards on 17 plays to draw close. The Bucs went 3-for-3 on fourth-down conversions in the drive, finally drawing closer on Brad Johnson's fourth-and-goal touchdown to Keenan McCardell and then the two-point conversion pass to Keyshawn Johnson.

It was 23–20 with 2:49 remaining. Plenty of time for Tampa Bay's top-ranked defense to make a stop, then position itself for a potential overtime-forcing field goal.

The Saints had third-and-8. Quarterback Aaron Brooks, with an injured shoulder, had his pads off. Jake Delhomme, the rusty replacement who had thrown one pass all season, then completed a pass to a diving Joe Horn, just beyond the yard marker.

Brad Johnson was under extreme pressure the entire game and was sacked four times.

Rice got to Aaron Brooks three times, setting a record for double-digit sacks in consecutive games.

First down. Game over.

The running game struggled again. Brad Johnson, who had been extremely efficient during Tampa Bay's five-game winning streak, worked under extreme pressure and was sacked four times. Still, he completed 28 of 44 for 276 dink-and-dunk yards.

The lasting memory? His ill-advised fourth-quarter interception on first-and-10 from the Tampa Bay 28-yard line, which set up John Carney's tack-on 48-yard field goal.

You can't pin this loss on Tampa Bay's defense, which surrendered just 238 total yards (a winning effort). The Bucs defense had four sacks, including three in the first quarter by Simeon Rice. When it really mattered, though, the Saints' Aaron Brooks had enough time to throw.

So now it's back to the brink. The breathing room is history. Now it's back to some urgency. Next: Atlanta at Tampa Bay. The Rock will be there.

The Cushion better be a long-lost memory . . . or else.

Joey Johnson

The Saints wrapped up McCardell until late in the game, when the Bucs' receiver scored to make it close.

With Lynch hurt, Howell wasted no time introducing himself to Vick, sacking him for a 6-yard loss.

Bucs 34, Falcons 10
December 8 at Tampa

Vicksburg Falls Again

John Lynch was injured. Strained neck. It was the first quarter and the Bucs' defense had lost a leader, a hitter, at the worst possible time. Across from them was the offense . . . and the quarterback . . . sweeping the NFL. In front of them was a game they had to win.

Lynch went to the side. His replacement, a fellow named John Howell, hopped in the huddle. He saw Derrick Brooks, who'd been flying, putting his stamp on the day. Brooks didn't say a word. Warren Sapp gave Howell big eyes and a big smile.

Howell nodded.

"Time to play," Howell said.

On the next play, Superman rolled out. John Howell, special teams guy, no name, rolled right with Atlanta Falcons wonder child Michael Vick. Then Howell rolled on top of him. Six-yard loss.

No time to waste. Time to play.

You knew it the moment Vick scrambled for the first time and Brooks raced after him. You knew it when Buc after Buc made play after play . . . on both sides of the ball. It was as complete a victory as we've seen from the Bucs in a long time.

Maybe New Orleans was a case of bad oysters. This was the main course. Here was a 34–10 beating of a team that hadn't been beaten in two

BUCS BONUS
ANOTHER VICTIM

GAME SUMMARY

Bucs	0	21	6	7 - 34
Falcons	0	3	0	7 - 10

Second Quarter

TB - Jurevicius 10 pass from B. Johnson (Gramatica kick), 11:12. Drive: 10 plays, 80 yards, 6:11.
TB - Jurevicius 13 pass from B. Johnson (Gramatica kick), 7:42. Drive: 2 plays, 10 yards, 0:31.
AT - FG Feely 30, 2:02. Drive: 11 plays, 48 yards, 5:35.
TB - McCardell 14 pass from B. Johnson (Gramatica kick), 0:34. Drive: 6 plays, 80 yards, 1:28.

Third Quarter

TB - FG Gramatica 42, 9:56. Drive: 10 plays, 55 yards, 5:04.
TB - FG Gramatica 21, 5:20. Drive: 8 plays, 66 yards, 3:21.

Fourth Quarter

AT - Crumpler 5 pass from Vick (Feely kick), 11:40. Drive: 8 plays, 86 yards, 4:49.
TB - McCardell 27 pass from B. Johnson (Gramatica kick), 8:31. Drive: 5 plays, 77 yards, 3:09.
A - 65,648

REACTION

"They won the war. Yeah, they won the war, but it's the second war of many during my career. This will be my rival."
—Michael Vick

NUMBERS GAME

Eight of Atlanta's 12 possessions ended in three-and-out or worse. The Falcons finished with 181 yards—103 in the second half after trailing 21-3.

BUCS HAVE VICK'S NUMBER

Atlanta quarterback Michael Vick averaged 272.4 yards of offense (213.4 passing, 59.0 rushing) in 13 games this season against opponents other than Tampa Bay. He averaged 89.0 yards of offense (81.0 passing, 8.0 rushing) in two games against the Bucs, who knocked him out with an injury in the third quarter of a 20-6 win at Atlanta on Oct. 6.

Opponents	Rushes	Yds.	TDs	Comp.-Att.	Yds.	TD	Int.
Vick vs. Bucs	6	16	0	16-37	162	1	1
Vick vs. others	106	767	8	215-384	2,774	15	7

NFC SOUTH STANDINGS

	W	L	T
Tampa Bay	10	3	0
New Orleans	9	4	0
Atlanta	8	4	1
Carolina	5	8	0

Jurevicius used his size to outjump and outmuscle the Falcons' Ray Buchanan for the second of his two touchdowns. Jurevicius had eight catches for 100 yards.

months, the up-and-comers from Vicksburg.

Well, Vicksburg fell.

"We didn't put a cape on his back," said Simeon Rice, the Bucs' rush monster. "The rest of the world did. We just took it off him."

Vick's talents were lost in a sea of red, where extraordinary is ordinary. Where discipline reigns. Where professionalism matters.

Consummate and convincing. No gimmicks, no gadgets. Just football that wouldn't let up. Just professionals minding to details while leveling a team on the rise. The Falcons were felled by professional ax swingers.

Professionals like Joe Jurevicius and Keenan McCardell, who caught two touchdowns apiece. Professionals like the quarterback who threw them the balls. Anybody still think Brad Johnson can't get a team to the Super Bowl? Give him 150 yards rushing and anything is possible.

It's possible because of the other professionals. Eleven of them start for the defense, and there's more where that came from. They are so special.

They know their business. They knew it as people reveled in Vick's highlight-reel talent.

"We laid around and let everyone figure out how we were going to stop Vick," Bucs nose tackle Booger McFarland said. "They never tried to figure out how they were going to stop us."

No tricks. No gimmicks. Just a defense that has been doing this for a long time.

A defense that seems to crank up even more when the big boys come to play. Vick was the big boy this time around.

They were a little sick of hearing about him.

We saw what happened.

What happened was discipline, starting up front. What happened was professionalism. What happened was Atlanta had 97 yards of offense until the last play of the third quarter.

The Bucs covered the other options and dared Vick to outrun them. Then they ran and ran, feeding off Brooks, who made 10 tackles, who was everywhere. Everyone else was right behind him. Vick, who ran for a quarterback-record 173 yards the week before, managed 16 yards in two games this season against the Bucs.

"I've never run up against a team like that," Vick said.

Special.

With three games left, it still can be special. As special as pros doing their jobs. As special, and as simple, as a nod from John Howell, the new guy in the huddle.

Time to play.

Martin Fennelly

Barber and the Bucs' defense again ripped the cape off Atlanta's Superman, limiting Vick to 9 yards rushing and 125 yards passing.

Sapp said, "Let's get the hell out of here," and the Bucs were soon on the plane after surviving another close call.

Bucs 23, Lions 20
December 15 at Detroit

Keep the Motor Running

They couldn't get to the buses fast enough. The buses that belched exhaust and gagged you like this game, the buses that went rumbling away from the Motor City.

To the airport. To the plane that took the Bucs above the clouds again, up there with all the possibilities, away from the cold, gray nightmare of what could have been in Detroit.

"Let's get the hell out of here," Warren Sapp said.

This was the "Let's Get the Hell Out of Here Game." All teams, including good ones, have them. The Bucs had one in Carolina earlier this season. They won that one.

And they won this one. They needed a whip and a chair and a late field goal, but they held off the Lions and clinched a playoff berth. They outlived the disaster that is a 10–3 team losing to a 3–10 team in December.

It was torture to watch. But then you realized the Bucs are in the playoffs.

And you looked around after they'd won and noticed the teams that hadn't. New Orleans, at home, had fallen to 3–10 Minnesota. Atlanta, at home, had lost to 4–9 Seattle.

The Bucs are a win away from a division title. After all that messing around, the truth was, of all things, just like Keyshawn Johnson said.

BUCS BONUS

A Big Step Forward

A Not-So-Pretty Victory Puts Bucs In Playoffs

The Bucs Got It Done, Won, And Got Out Of Town Fast

Game 14

BUCS 23, LIONS 20

Gramatica's fourth-quarter field goal silenced the Lions and earned the Bucs a playoff berth.

Alstott capped a 96-yard drive with a 1-yard rumble to the end zone. It gave the Bucs a short-lived 10-0 lead.

"One more and we get to put on the hats."

It didn't matter how it looked. It didn't matter because this is the stretch where winning means momentum, with or without style points. It didn't matter because it is December and the Eagles and Packers won and the Bucs kept up the drag race.

One more and they get NFC South hats.

"There's not a lot of teams in the NFL that have 11 wins," Gruden said. "I don't really give a rat's behind how we get them, as long as we get them."

This isn't the 7–6 Bucs squeaking one out to keep playoff dreams alive. This is 11–3 with bigger. There's no sense here that this game will linger. It didn't matter how it looked.

Get it done. Get it won. And get out.

The Bucs nearly lost to a team with the NFL's 31st-best offense and 27th-best defense.

The Bucs nearly lost to a team that was without four starters, including their running game, James Stewart.

Then Lions quarterback Joey Harrington left with an irregular heartbeat.

A lot of other Lion hearts beat regular, proud and regular.

The Bucs nearly lost to backup quarterback Mike McMahon.

The Bucs nearly lost to two guys they'd never heard of, Aveion Cason and Rafael Cooper, who together had rushed for 24 yards in Detroit's first 12 games. They gained 112 against Tampa Bay.

The Bucs nearly lost despite a 96-yard touchdown drive that gave them a 10–0 lead.

The Bucs nearly lost even after Shelton Quarles intercepted a pass, Brad Johnson hit Keyshawn for 30 yards and Michael Pittman scored his first touchdown of the season for a 20–13 lead.

The Lions scored 24 seconds later. Somebody named Eddie Drummond brought the kick back 91 yards. McMahon scored on the next play. It was 20–20.

Yes, the Bucs nearly lost. But they didn't.

Martin Gramatica kicked another field goal, the defense held, the offense ran out the clock and the Bucs ran for the bus. They counted their blessings and remembered why home field matters in the playoffs.

"It's the road," Sapp said. "New Orleans couldn't win here in Detroit. Philly lost in Jacksonville."

The Bucs haven't let that happen this season. That's one reason why there is still no ceiling on this postseason, no matter what anyone says. Just ask Gruden.

"Hell's bells, I'm so tired of hearing the god-dang experts tell me we can't win a game when it's cold, we can't win on the road, and damn sure if we go to Philadelphia, we have no chance.

"We're going to fight. We've proven that."

They got the hell out of Detroit.

One more and they get to put on the hats.

Martin Fennelly

Mike McMahon, who replaced Joey Harrington, perplexed Sapp and his teammates and nearly pulled off the upset.

The low point of the season for Keyshawn, Pittman and McCardell. For one night, the "paper champions" label fit.

Game 15

Steelers 17, **Bucs 7**
December 23 at Tampa

A Pitiful Night

On second thought, a road play-off game may not be such a bad thing. After all, with one trip remaining, the Bucs were 5–2 away from Raymond James Stadium, and their Monday night performance did little to suggest that playing at home will provide a playoff edge.

Although they were crowned NFC South champions the day before thanks to a New Orleans loss, the Bucs did nothing to erase Pittsburgh safety Lee Flowers' claim that they are "paper champions."

"They jumped out on us and we had no answer for them," Warren Sapp said. "We kept getting close to the end zone but we couldn't mount anything. We just need to take our [loss] like a man."

By losing, the Bucs turned the NFC's battle for homefield advantage throughout the play-offs into a two-team race involving Green Bay and Philadelphia.

Although they did not surrender a point from the second quarter on, the Bucs' defense started slowly, allowing all the points the Steelers needed to end Tampa Bay's two-game winning streak in the first 11 minutes.

The offense, which sat out Brad Johnson because of a severe back bruise, also struggled at the outset, turning

GAME SUMMARY

Bucs	0	0	7	7	-7
Steelers	17	0	0	0	- 17

First Quarter

P – Randel El 11 pass from Maddox (Reed kick), 12:01. Drive: 6 plays, 81 yards, 2:59.

P – C. Scott 30 yd. Interception return (Reed kick), 11:10.

P – FG Reed 26, 4:24. Drive: 9 plays, 67 yards, 2:20.

Fourth Quarter

TB – K. Johnson 18 pass from R. Johnson (Gramatica kick), 1:14. Drive: 9 plays, 67 yards, 2:20.

A - 65,684

REACTION

"They felt very confident, but please don't bully us. That's the last thing that a team needs to do to us if they think they're going to win the game." —Pittsburgh's Lee Flowers

NUMBERS GAME

Keyshawn Johnson passed the 1,000-yard receiving mark for the second straight year and the fourth time in his career. He finished the season with 1,088 yards.

BUCS ON MONDAY NIGHT

The Bucs are 6-5 all-time on ABC's marquee game (5-2 at home, 1-3 on the road):

Date	Result	Site
Oct. 6, 1980	Bears 23, Bucs 0	Chicago
Nov. 29, 1982	Bucs 23, Dolphins 17	Tampa
Dec. 12, 1983	Packers 12, Bucs 9	Tampa
Dec. 28, 1998	Lions 27, Bucs 6	Detroit
Dec. 7, 1998	Bucs 24, Packers 22	Tampa
Dec. 6, 1999	Bucs 24, Vikings 17	Tampa
Oct. 9, 2000	Vikings 30, Bucs 23	Minneapolis
Dec. 16, 2000	Bucs 38, Rams 35	Tampa
Nov. 26, 2001	Bucs 24, Rams 17	St. Louis
Sept. 23, 2002	Bucs 26, Rams 14	Tampa
Dec. 23, 2002	Steelers 17, Bucs 7	Tampa

NFC SOUTH STANDINGS

	W	L	T
Tampa Bay	11	4	0
Atlanta	9	5	1
New Orleans	9	6	0
Carolina	6	9	0

the ball over and surrendering a touchdown on its second play from scrimmage.

Flowers' comments after last year's game led to bad blood in pregame warm-ups, when Pittsburgh's Joey Porter and Tampa Bay's Nate Webster got into a shouting match. A few minutes later, the Steelers' Jerome Bettis shoved Sapp as the Bucs' star came out of the locker room.

"We don't like them, they don't like us," said Pittsburgh's Hines Ward.

After the opening kickoff, the Steelers threw the first punch.

The Steelers built a 17–0 first-quarter lead on a Tommy Maddox touchdown pass, a Chad Scott interception return for a TD and a Jeff Reed field goal.

Scott's return came after King made a questionable decision to force a pass to Keyshawn Johnson along the right sideline. It was not, however, the Bucs' most questionable decision.

After a pregame shove of Sapp, Pittsburgh's Jerome Bettis gave Lynch a stiff arm.

Barber and the Bucs eventually corralled the Steelers' Tommy Maddox, but the damage already had been done.

That was made two series later, after Reed had increased the Steelers' edge to 17–0, when Gruden took three points off the board by accepting a penalty that nullified a 50-yard Martin Gramatica field goal. Four plays later, Alstott fumbled at the Pittsburgh 7.

"I wouldn't do anything differently there," Gruden said. "Unfortunately, it backfired on me."

Roy Cummings

Gramatica went five-for-five in the chill of
Champaign to ice a first-round bye.

Game 16

Bucs 15, Bears 0
December 29 at Champaign, Illinois

Very Cool Stuff

Not this time. The Bucs would not give it back again. Twice they said bye-bye to a bye. On this day, destiny fell into their hands once more. They grabbed it, and who knows what else, by the throat.

Not even the thermometer could stare them down. Or the thought of life without Brad Johnson. How could the scoreboard say different? The Bucs' defense would not let it. The Packers had lost earlier in the day. And the Bucs would not let another chance escape.

The Chicago Bears were more ghosts than galloping in Red Grange's old house. The Bucs did what was needed in a 15–0 win, earning the No. 2 seed and a first-round bye in the postseason. It did not need to be pretty. Five Martin Gramatica field goals seemed like a mighty onslaught. The Bucs' defense made it so. with its second shutout this season.

By any degree— and there were less than 40 of them when the game began (talk about ghosts)— this was a giant leap for Buc-kind. With teeth chattering, with rumors about Johnson's injured back howling like the wind, they regained the high ground, or at least enough of it to stay off Green Bay tundra if it comes to that.

GAME SUMMARY

Bucs	3	6	0	6 - 15
Bears	0	0	0	0 - 0

First Quarter
TB - FG Gramatica 33, 3:09. Drive: 4 plays, 3 yards, 0:25.

Second Quarter
TB - FG Gramatica 30, 3:22. Drive: 12 plays, 48 yards, 6:48.
TB - FG Gramatica 32, 0:02. Drive: 5 plays, 20 yards, 0:58.

Fourth Quarter
TB - FG Gramatica 33, 13:12. Drive: 15 plays, 65 yards, 8:10.
TB - FG Gramatica 26, 7:01. Drive: 10 plays, 40 yards, 6:04.
A - 44,106

REACTION
"We finally got that Abominable Snowman off our backs. ... All this means really is that people will now say we're 1-21 when it's 39 or colder. It won't mean anything until we're dominant in this kind of weather." —Warren Sapp

SEEING THE FOOT IN FOOTBALL
Martin Gramatica kicked five field goals against Chicago, marking the fifth time he has kicked four or more in a game. This was his second four-plus effort on the road.

Date	Opponent	FG Lengths	Results
Nov. 21, 99	Atlanta	24, 26, 50, 53	Win, 19-10
Oct. 19, 00	Detroit	50, 43, 27, 55	Lose, 28-14
Dec. 23, 01	New Orleans	20, 24, 32, 27	Win, 48-21
Oct. 27, 02	at Carolina	32, 52, 53, 47	Win, 12-9
Dec. 29, 02	at Chicago	33, 30, 32, 33, 26	Win, 15-0

NFC SOUTH STANDINGS

	W	L	T
Tampa Bay	12	4	0
Atlanta	9	6	1
New Orleans	9	7	0
Carolina	7	9	0

Yes, the Eagles are out there. But this wasn't about them. It was about the Bucs, who did what they had to do. There were snow drifts in the bleachers at ancient Memorial Stadium. The Bucs warmed to the task.

After all the worrying, the doom and gloom lifted and the Bucs had won 12 games, more than any Bucs team had in the regular season.

We all know that Jon Gruden was brought here to do more than this, that the postseason is when we start keeping score.

But give his team credit.

Think of what could have happened. Think of the Saints, who faded away. Better yet, think of the Dolphins, who couldn't find their way into the playoffs with 1,800-yard rusher Ricky Williams.

Imagine if the Bucs had lost to the Bears, to Chicago quarterback Henry Burris, who entered the game having completed 11 NFL passes, whose last professional start came for a team in Saskatchewan. Imagine if the Bucs had dropped this ball.

Rob Johnson got another start and managed the offense well against a wounded Bears team.

It was sweet home Chicago for Alstott, who ran for 42 yards. Pittman added 90 yards as the Bucs' running game was impressive for the third time in four games.

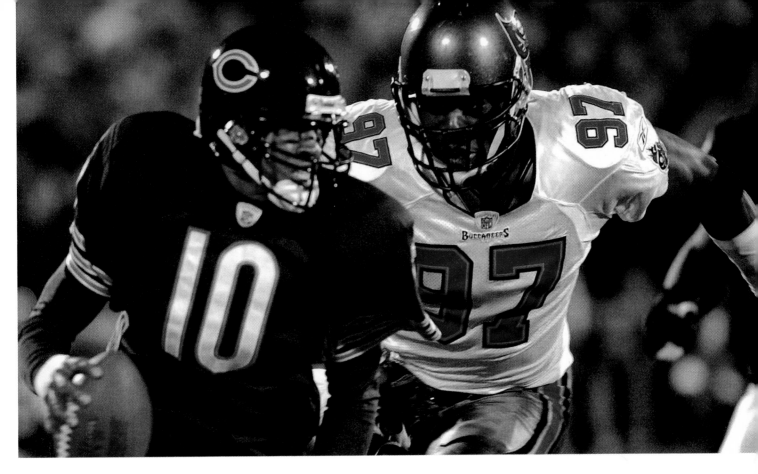

Well, quit imagining.

And dream a little dream.

The Bears threatened once when the game was in doubt, and Burris was picked off by Derrick Brooks. Kelly had two picks. Sapp, playing hurt, had seven tackles. This defense, this defense, this defense. It would not lose this game.

Nor would Rob Johnson, and for now that will do. Michael Pittman finally looked as strong as his biceps with 90 yards on the ground. For the third time in four games, the running game was there. All week long . . . all season long . . . Gruden told his team they would get what they deserved.

When the Bucs came into the locker room, the Packers were on the television, losing their first-round bye. Players looked at each other. Did they deserve this?

"We made it so," Brooks said.

And so they did. When it was over. They could see their breath and knew a little bit more of the old Bucs was dead.

"How cold was it?" Kelly asked.

You told him 38 degrees at kickoff, a record low for a Bucs victory. You told Brooks. Who knows what this team will do in coming weeks. Brooks knew only one thing.

"We can make any history we want," he said.

Then he smiled.

Definite warming trend.

Martin Fennelly

Rice helped to pressure Henry Burris into four interceptions. The Bears' QB, making his first NFL start, threw for only 78 yards.

By opening up a big lead, the Bucs forced San Francisco to abandon its running game. The result: Garrison Hearst and the 49ers did not even get a sniff of the end zone.

Bucs 31, 49ers 6
January 12 at Tampa

A Banner Day

The victors stood in a tunnel before it began. Raymond James Stadium was alive with 65,000 flags, some red, some white, handed out to mark the way for the Buccaneers.

"I hope they put that in the Madden video game next year," Bucs cornerback Dwight Smith said. "It was an incredible sight."

They weren't so bad themselves.

The Bucs could not have had a more perfect afternoon. The people who should have been waving the white flags were the ones who needed them most, the 49ers, who fell 31–6 to a team bound for the NFC Championship Game in Philadelphia.

Could this be the way to San Diego and a Super Bowl?

What else can you think when the Bucs score the most dominant playoff win in franchise history? What about a defense that shut down the 49ers, beginning with 49ers receiver Terrell Owens, the fabulous T.O.?

R.I.P.

What about Jon Gruden's first playoff game as Bucs head coach? He has the Bucs in their third title game, just like that. This is why he was brought here. He looked like he was worth every dollar and draft pick the Glazers paid for him. With interest. Great interest.

BUCS BONUS

MONDAY, JANUARY 13, 2003 • THE TAMPA TRIBUNE • TBO.COM

ONE STEP AWAY

FLAGS ARE FINAL HURDLE ON ROAD TO SUPER BOWL

Bucs 31, 49ers 6

Brad Leads Band Of Bucs, Has Eye Patch To Prove It

GAME SUMMARY

Bucs	7	21	3	0 -	31
49ers	3	3	0	0 -	6

First Quarter

TB - Alstott 2 run (Gramatica kick), 6:34. Drive: 12 plays, 74 yards, 5:15.

SF - FG Chandler 24, 0:17. Drive: 12 plays, 63 yards, 6:12

Second Quarter

TB - Jurevicius 20 pass from B. Johnson (Gramatica kick), 9:27. Drive: 11 plays, 77 yards, 5:50.

SF - FG Chandler 40, 8:31. Drive: 5 plays, 24 yards, 0:56.

TB - Dudley 12 pass from B. Johnson (Gramatica kick), 7:24. Drive: 2 plays, 52 yards, 1:07.

TB - Alstott 2 run (Gramatica kick), 0:50. Drive: 4 plays, 24 yards, 1:10.

Third Quarter

TB - FG Gramatica 19, 8:28. Drive: 10 plays, 36 yards, 6:16.
A - 65,559

REACTION

"We realize we've got our hands full, but we're going to get on the plane and we're going to go, and we'll play any place, whether it be in the Vet or the Walt Whitman Bridge. We're going to be there." —Jon Gruden, on playing at Philadelphia in the NFC Championship Game

REACTION

"They thrive on coming back. We thrive on burying people. You've been in our arena. We've already dug the hole, now all we have to do is drag you to it and put the dirt on you. It's pretty simple after we've dug that hole." —Warren Sapp

REACTION

"You always want to get another crack at somebody who has beaten you. We've lost to them three times the last three years in Philadelphia. We would like to go up there and close down the Vet with nice memories." —Keyshawn Johnson

NUMBERS GAME

Led by a pair of turnovers recovered by the NFL Defensive Player of the Year, Derrick Brooks, (fumble recovery, interception) and Dwight Smith, (fumble recovery, interception), the Bucs forced a playoff team-record five turnovers.

FAMILIAR TERRITORY

Most playoff appearances in the past six years:

Team	No.
Tampa Bay	5
Miami	5
Green Bay	4
Minnesota	4
San Francisco	4

"Nice flags," Gruden said.

It was 28–6 at halftime. Clearly, the 49ers left their heart in San Francisco. This was a mass grave.

The Bucs did the burying.

Bucs general manager Rich McKay said, "For the fans and people who stick by this franchise through thin and thinner, it's awfully nice to see them get rewarded with a home playoff win and not one they had to have a heart attack watching."

Even bad turned to beautiful.

The crowd gasped when Bucs quarterback Brad Johnson, finally back from a back injury, went down with a nasty gash to the head. But the crowd made a blood roar as Johnson pumped his fist while being carted from the field. He returned to finish with 196 yards passing and two touchdowns.

And there was that defense, led by the league's defensive MVP, Derrick Brooks. It held San Francisco to 222 total yards and Owens, a dazzler who this season autographed a touchdown ball while still in the end zone, to just five catches for 35 yards.

"We're 60 minutes away from the greatest show on earth," Bucs defensive lineman Warren Sapp said.

A Super Bowl.

"There's a bounce with this team, and I've said that since training camp. You've got to start with Jon, because he's about juice."

With an interception, fumble recovery and half a sack, Brooks enhanced his reputation as the NFL's biggest playmaker at linebacker.

Red and white flags - 65,000 strong — were flying at Raymond James Stadium and making quite an impression on the Bucs

Meanwhile, silver-haired royalty was ushered down a hall to see Gruden. It was Bill Walsh, the former 49ers head coach who won three Super Bowls for San Francisco, designing offenses Gruden grew up dreaming about.

Walsh, now a 49ers consultant, wanted to see the kid. Their wizard visited our wizard.

"He offered me a job!" Walsh joked.

"That was one of the greatest moments of my football career," Gruden said of the meeting.

So was this game.

On to Philly.

"We'll play anyplace, the Vet or the Walt Whitman Bridge," Gruden said. "We're going to be there."

Jon Gruden's eyes narrowed. No retreat. No surrender.

Not a white flag in sight.

Feel the juice?

Martin Fennelly

In the red zone, the Bucs went to Alstott, who responded with two touchdowns. He was the first Buc to cross the goal line in the postseason since 1999.

When Barber raced to the end zone,
the Vet crowd went silent.

Bucs 27, Eagles 10
January 19 at Philadelphia

The Last Laugh

en walked on the moon on this day.

It didn't matter that the moon was 240,000 miles away.

The Bucs are going to the Super Bowl.

It was early evening, and the art of fiction was as dead as the Philadelphia Eagles and their arthritic ball yard. In the last football game at Veterans Stadium, the Bucs burned the place to the ground, along with every demon that ever haunted them.

The National Football Conference champions' buses roared to life. The horns would be pounded all the way to the Philadelphia airport, a honking brotherly reminder to Eagles fans that their city did not belong to them until the Bucs handed it back.

There were no more ghosts. The only history that mattered was the history just made, winning 27-10 against the team they couldn't beat in a place they couldn't win, surrounded by a chill and a crowd and a world that didn't give them a snowball's chance in—you know, that place that has now frozen over.

The Bucs are going to the Super Bowl.

There would be a crowd waiting in Tampa.

They've been waiting 27 years. This was their night, too.

Wave your flags. Bang your pots and pans. Make like

BUCS BONUS

SWEET REVENGE

The Bucs exorcise their demons at Veterans Stadium, pounding the Eagles 27-10 to advance to their first Super Bowl, a showdown with Coach Jon Gruden's former team, the Oakland Raiders.

GAME SUMMARY

Bucs	10	7	3	7 - 27
Eagles	7	3	0	0 - 10

First Quarter
P - Staley 20 run, (Akers kick), 14:08. Drive: 2 plays, 26 yards, 0:52.
TB - FG Gramatica 48, 10:01. Drive: 9 plays, 37 yards, 4:10.
TB - Alstott 1 run (Gramatica kick), 0:40. Drive: 7 plays, 96 yards, 3:15.

Second Quarter
P - FG Akers 30, 8:04. Drive: 8 plays, 26 yards, 3:53.
TB - K. Johnson 9 pass from B. Johnson (Gramatica kick), 2:28. Drive: 12 plays, 80 yards, 5:36.

Third Quarter
TB - FG Gramatica 27, 1:02. Drive: 8 plays, 43 yards, 3:35.

Fourth Quarter
TB - Barber 92 yard interception return, 3:12.
A - 66,713

REACTION
"Ronde Barber was all over the place. I don't think I've seen a DB make as many plays in one game as he did."
— defensive coordinator Monte Kiffin

NUMBERS GAME
Defensive hero Ronde Barber forced a fumble, broke up four passes, had three tackles and returned an interception 92 yards for the game-clinching touchdown. Those were the first fourth-quarter points scored by a Bucs team in the postseason.

BUCS VS. EAGLES
The Eagles lead the regular-season series 5-3, but the postseason series is tied 2-2.

Year	Winner	Score	Site
2002	Bucs,	27-10*	Philadelphia
2002	Eagles,	20-10	Philadelphia
2001	Eagles,	31-9***	Philadelphia
2001	Eagles,	17-13	Tampa
2000	Eagles,	21-3***	Philadelphia
1999	Bucs,	19-5	Philadelphia
1995	Bucs,	21-6	Philadelphia
1991	Bucs,	14-13	Tampa
1988	Eagles,	41-14	Tampa
1981	Eagles,	20-10	Philadelphia
1979	Bucs,	24-17**	Tampa
1977	Eagles,	13-3	Philadelphia

* NFC Championship Game
** NFC Wild Card Playoff Game
*** NFC Divisional Playoff Game

You Gotta Hand It Too Brad

What, you thought a little thing like sub-freezing cold was going to bother Brad Johnson? A football that believed it was an ice cube was supposed to send him into a wounded-duck wobble? Get real.

This is what the playoffs will do to you: They take a thin-blooded Southern boy and turn him into a blast furnace.

Against the Eagles and a wind-chill factor of 16 degrees, Johnson was hotter than that Miller Lite commercial. Facing a defense that in past meetings had come at him like metal to a magnet, Johnson completed 20 of 33 passes for 259 yards, one touchdown and a single interception. Almost as important, he was not sacked.

But before you can have a hot hand, you must first have a warm hand.

For the NFC Championship Game, Johnson's famous game-day wardrobe changes included new sets of quarterback gloves. Johnson often struggles when attempting to throw cold or wet footballs. So he took to the new fashion statement like, well, hand to glove.

The idea of using the new-wave quarterback mittens was first mentioned during training camp by Gruden. "Next thing I know, he's got a bucket of water out there, dipping the ball in the water," Johnson said.

"Yeah, I've done a lot of research on those gloves," said Gruden, a one-time quarterback at the University of Dayton. "I was not a very good passer myself and could not throw the ball at all when it was wet or cold. I picked up these gloves and I miraculously could throw the ball like Brad Johnson.

"We tried these gloves and he spun the ball great on the practice field back in Tampa. He asked me if he should wear them and I said, 'If you don't wear them, I'm going to strap you down and put them on.' It was a factor. It was a really positive thing for Brad."

Mick Elliott

The Vet, the Eagles, the cold and history were stacked against the Bucs, but the NFC champions exorcised all of their Philadelphia demons.

Chucky, the man of a thousand faces who delivered the game of a lifetime. Go Jon Gruden crazy, folks. Nothing is silly. No one will laugh at you. Or your football team.

The Bucs are going to the Super Bowl.

Men walked on the moon. They kissed and hugged and cried and remembered those who went before them, men who people laughed at.

The Bucs' defense sealed the day. There was poetry in that. Barber stepped in front of a Donovan McNabb pass. It was 92 yards to the end zone. Barber ran in total silence.

"You couldn't hear a sound," John Lynch said. "The stadium noise stopped. There was that sweet silence. There was nothing to say."

This was about a franchise that had finally risen so far above its deep, dark orange past that there was nothing else to do but call them champions.

This wasn't just for them. This was for all those old Bucs, men like Richard "Batman" Wood and Paul Gruber, who were honorary captains Sunday. Old Bucs who'd fought the good fight but never had their hands raised in true victory.

This was for teams that couldn't win, teams in the creamsicle uniforms, teams with the winking pirate on their helmets, teams of Mr. C and Sam Wyche and Booker Reese. And for fans who suffered those days at Tampa Stadium. It wasn't the heat, it was the humiliation. The Yucks.

When Alstott ended a 96-yard drive with a touchdown off left end, Eagles fans realized the Bucs came to play.

No more.

They began the game with their backs against the wall. Then those backs were in the wall. Philadelphia broke off a kickoff return and scored a touchdown two plays later. The game wasn't a minute old.

Last year, in a similar situation, they rolled over and quit. These Bucs would not quit. They would not roll over. Later, Warren Sapp sat at his locker. His right eye was nearly swollen shut. It took five stitches to stop the bleeding after he caught a finger above the eye.

His vision was blurred, but he still saw things clearly.

"We wrote our own history out there," he said.

This day really began as a short pass from Brad Johnson, who journeyed far and wide, without much notice, to this moment. The ball was caught by Joe Jurevicius. If this game was about heart, his was among the biggest.

Jurevicius arrived in Philadelphia a day later than his teammates. He missed practice during the week. His wife,

It didn't take long for Kenyatta Walker to get the word out: Tampa Bay was going to the Super Bowl.

Glazer and Gruden shared the NFC's Halas Trophy, then the boss gave his genius a kiss.

Meagan, just gave birth to their first child, a boy named Michael William. But there were complications.

Now Joe Jurevicius ran across the middle and down the sideline, 71 yards, deep into Philadelphia territory. The Bucs scored a few plays later. This Sunday would be different.

"Joe was really moving," John Lynch said. "I bet his son had something to do with that."

There would be no stopping this team. The Bucs won physical battles all day. And there was one of the world's 50 most beautiful game plans by the man in the visor.

Gruden outcoached Philadelphia's Andy Reid all afternoon. He found mismatches. He used motion and play action and spread the ball around, and let the record state that the winning points were scored on a touchdown by Keyshawn Johnson.

Go figure.

Turns out Jon Gruden was a steal.

He was brought here to put the Bucs over the top.

When it was over, Gruden mentioned the man who coached before him, Tony Dungy. The man who first made people stop laughing at the Bucs. Him and men like Hardy Nickerson. A little piece of this victory belongs to a whole lot of people.

It was right that the defense sealed it. It had first lifted this franchise from the football netherworld. Now it had dominated the Eagles. And when it came time for Gruden to get doused from a bucket, the men behind the bucket were Lynch, Sapp and Derrick Brooks. That was right, too.